The Skit Book

The Skit Book

101 Skits from Kids

Margaret Read MacDonald

Illustrations by Marie-Louise Scull

www.augusthouse.com

August House Publishers, Inc.
ATLANTA

Published by August House Publishers, Inc.
3500 Piedmont Road NE, Suite 310, Atlanta, GA 30305
www.augusthouse.com
Originally published 1990 by Linnet Books
First August House edition, 2006
Printed in the United States of America

10 9 8 7 6 5 4 3 2   PB

LIBRARY OF CONGRESS CATALOGING-IN-PUBLICATION DATA

THE SKIT BOOK : 101 SKITS FROM KIDS / [COLLECTED BY] MARGARET READ
MACDONALD. -- 1ST AUGUST HOUSE ED.
        P. CM.
ORIGINALLY PUBLISHED: HAMDEN, CONN. : LINNET BOOKS, 1990.
INCLUDES BIBLIOGRAPHICAL REFERENCES AND INDEX.
ISBN-13: 978-0-87483-785-8 (PBK.)
ISBN-10: 0-87483-785-5 (PBK.)
1. AMATEUR PLAYS. 2. CHILDREN'S WRITINGS, AMERICAN. I. MACDONALD,
MARGARET READ, 1940-

PN6120.S8S65 2006
812'.0410892--DC22

2006040334

The paper used in this publication meets the minimum requirements of the
American National Standard for Information Sciences—Permanence of
Paper for Printed Library Materials, ANSI Z39.48–1984.

For Jenny and Julie MacDonald
and all the great kids at
Youth Theatre Northwest

Contents

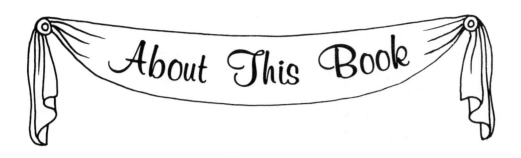

About This Book

These skits were collected from kids I know. I have tried to include the skits they liked best. To tell the truth, I wanted to leave out the stuff in the "Grossies" section. I thought those skits were pretty disgusting. But then I realized if this was to be a book "by kids and for kids" I'd have to leave them in. And then the kids made me drop some of MY favorite skits . . . they said they were just too dumb!

These skits are really simple to perform. Don't worry about costumes and props. Whatever you can scrounge up in fifteen minutes should do. Don't worry about learning lines. Just ad lib, clown, and keep it moving.

All the skits in this book are planned for any number of performers. If you have lots of kids in your group, just add characters to the skit. If you have only a few kids, let some play more than one part.

I hope you enjoy these skits as much as the kids in Seattle, Washington, who helped me make this book. These skits are really a kind of folklore. Everybody who uses them changes them. So just use the ideas as a starting point. Change everything to suit yourself and your friends.

WHAT IS A SKIT?

This book is offering only one kind of skit: the "camp skit." I call it a "camp skit" because that is where it has been most often performed — but skits are used in schools, churches, day camps, recreation centers, and heaven knows where else. I heard of one Alaskan cannery where the summer workers hold skit nights to entertain themselves; and skit nights are popular entertainments at senior centers and on cruise ships, too. So adults seem to enjoy these as much as kids!

These "camp skits"

- Are short.
- Require only the sort of prop and costume you can scare up in a few minutes.
- Have no lines to learn. You just ad lib them.
- Are based on one humorous idea or punch line.
- Can use any number of actors.
- Are often based on ideas from a skit performance seen somewhere else.
- Are performed without much rehearsal.
- Are performed by a group of friends, for a group of people you know.

WHERE DO SKITS COME FROM?

Skits are an interesting form of folklore. They are usually made up by a group, not by one person. Each skit is based on one humorous idea. Of course, one person usually comes up with the skit idea, but then the group takes it over and everyone throws in suggestions to build it into a really funny performance.

Most of these skit ideas come from people who remember seeing a great skit at some gathering, often summer camp. Skit ideas are passed in this way from camp to camp, but the same skit also pops up at the school talent show, at day camp — everywhere you see skits performed. Since they are passed around by word of mouth, and since they are changed by every group that uses them, they are true folklore!

Skits get better when a group of really clever kids gets ahold of them. And they can deteriorate into real bombs at times. Sometimes kids don't quite remember the way a skit should go and strange things result. This happened at one camp with "The Empty Heads" (skit #44). In this skit each actor pretends to spit water into the ear of the person next to her. The first person drinks the water from a glass . . . the last person spits a mouthful of water into the glass. Of course, this last person should have her mouth full of water from the start, and the glass that passes down the line is really empty. But one group didn't remember how the skit should go. In their performance each person wound up rinsing her mouth with the SAME water from the glass. Now that *is* gross! Maybe this book will help you remember some of those skits you saw in the past and liked. Maybe it will prevent some bungles.

I hope you won't rely *too* heavily on this book for ideas. Even as I type this, kids are probably sitting around somewhere concocting great new skits that will be even *better* than these. And if they are good enough, somebody will remember them and carry them off to another audience next year. Folklore is like that: it just keeps recreating itself.

HOW DID SKITS ORIGINATE?

Although the performance of dramatic skits has an ancient history, the use of the simple "camp skit" seems to stem mainly from the first part of this century. The first youth summer camps and recreation centers were just being started then, and skits were a fun activity. Some of our most popular skits today — the melodramas, the mixed body parts, the operation skits — were popular as early as the 1920s. Many books about skits were published between 1920 and 1950. Several of them are included in the bibliography here.

But even before that time, families and friends enjoyed getting together to perform "parlor entertainments." Before the days of radio and TV folks had to make their own entertainment in the evening. Pantomimes and dramatic skits were popular, although they didn't take quite the same form as our camp skits today.

The idea of folks getting together to put on a short, silly play for their friends isn't anything new. In England people used to dress up in costumes at Christmas time and go around to their neighbors performing humorous skits. Their skits followed a sort of script, though. This was called Mumming. Similar short humorous plays which required little rehearsal were performed by workmen's guilds as long ago as the Middle Ages! My favorite historical example of a skit is in Shakespeare's play, *A Midsummer Night's Dream*. In that play there is a scene in which several workmen get together to put on a silly play of their own. Their antics are really funny. You might like to read that scene or see the play sometime.

Whatever the actual origins of our skits, they are certainly a popular item today. And YOU are a part of the skit tradition. Maybe you will add a bit to a skit, or create a new skit idea, which will be passed on and turn up in somebody else's skit book fifty years from now!

Skits with Trick Endings

This section includes many "classic" skits such as "The Reporter at the Bridge" and "J.C. Penney's Clothes." Though skits are often created from jokes, many of these "trick ending" skits clearly originated as camp skits. These skits are sometimes written down and mimeographed for distribution among camp leaders, but they seem to pass from camp to camp mainly through the memories of the campers and counselors.

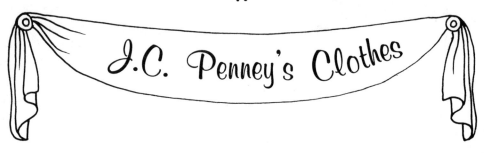

J.C. Penney's Clothes

CAST: Salesperson, J.C. Penney, any number of shoppers.

SCENE: Clothing store. A curtain behind which J.C. Penney hides.

ACTION: Shoppers enter one by one and ask for items of clothing. "I'd like to buy a shirt." Salesperson says "Certainly!" and calls behind curtain, "We need a SHIRT up front." An arm holds out a shirt. The salesperson shows it off proudly to the customer. "This is J.C. Penney's shirt. I'm sure you'll like it." Shopper buys it and leaves. Other customers come in and ask for a belt . . . tie . . . pants . . . shoes . . . hat . . . socks . . . etc. The arm holds out the item each time, after a pause, and the clerk brags, "This is J.C. Penney's belt!"

ENDING: The last shopper says, "I'd like to buy a pair of shorts." The curtain shakes and J.C. Penney races out through the audience shrieking, wearing only a pair of undershorts.

Shopper: "Who was THAT?"
Salesperson: "That was J.C. Penney."

Variants

Use any brand name you like for the clothing, such as Calvin Klein, Liz Claiborne, or Jay Jacobs.

2.

The Reporter at the Bridge

CAST: A reporter contemplating suicide. Several people passing by.

SCENE: A bridge.

ACTION: A reporter comes onstage and stands by the railing of an imaginary bridge. The reporter says it is impossible to get a good story nowadays. The reporter has given up and plans to jump off the bridge and end it all. Just as the reporter is about to leap, another person comes by. When this person hears the reporter's sad tale he tells the story of his own woes and decides to jump with the reporter. Another person comes by and listens to their sad tales. She decides to jump too. Repeat this until all your actors are onstage. Each can make up his own story of despair.

ENDING: The reporter suggests that on the count of three everyone leap from the bridge together. All do, except for the reporter. The reporter races offstage shouting, "WOW! What a STORY!"

3.

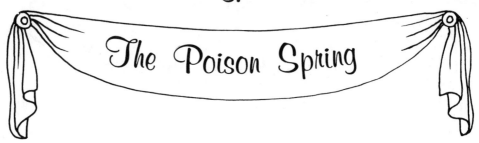

The Poison Spring

CAST: Any number of people who are dying of thirst.

SCENE: A spring with a bucket and a dipper.

ACTION: One by one people stagger or crawl onstage calling for water. Each reaches the bucket, takes a drink from the dipper, and dies. Ham up the dying as much as you like. There should be real water in the dipper, but not in the bucket. Spill some as you drink so the audience knows it is real water. You might want to rig dippers full of water for each drinker, so there is plenty of water to slop around.

ENDING: The second-to-last person starts to drink from the bucket. Just then the last person comes in, sees the dead bodies, and rushes up to snatch the bucket away. "Don't drink that—IT'S POISON!!!" This person throws the contents of the bucket out into the audience! The bucket itself contains only rice or confetti, which spills all over the audience. Only the dippers had water in them, and they lie around the floor by the dead bodies now. Of course the audience thinks the bucket is full of water and gets quite a shock.

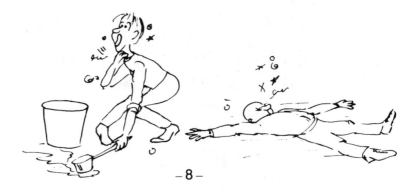

4.

Is It Time Yet?

CAST: Person with watch. Any number of waiting people.

SCENE: A waiting room with a row of chairs.

ACTION: Everyone has right leg crossed over left. Everyone is reading a newspaper. The person on one end asks the person sitting next to her, "Is it time yet?" The question is passed down the line. The person at the other end looks at her watch and says, "No. Not yet." This answer is passed back down the line. The person on the end waits awhile and then asks again, "Is it TIME yet?" The question is passed down and comes back with the answer, "No, not yet!" Repeat this, adding variety by asking the question in a bored way, an angry way, an impatient way, etc. Another approach is to carry it out in a detached, deadpan manner.

ENDING: The watch holder finally responds. "Yes. It's TIME." When this answer has been passed back down the line, all look at one another . . . then everyone crosses legs in the opposite direction and refolds the newspaper, in unison. All sigh. And the skit is over.

5.

The Pickpocket Contest

CAST: Several pickpockets. An announcer.

SCENE: Pickpocket competition.

ACTION: The announcer introduces the greatest pickpockets in the world to compete for the championship title. "Would the first two pickpockets please take their places? Get ready. Get set. Go!" Two pickpockets cross the stage from opposite directions. They meet in the middle and stop to chat briefly, patting each other on the shoulder, chest, leg, etc. Each walks on, then turns to the audience and holds up a stolen object. One has a pocket watch; one has a ballpoint pen. Repeat this with as many competitors as you like. Increase the level of pickpocket difficulty each time.

ENDING: The announcer says that two semi-finalists have been chosen to compete for the championship title. They take their place and begin the encounter. As they walk away from each other, one holds up the other's belt. The announcer and other pickpockets cheer. But the second pickpocket suddenly whips out a pair of boxer shorts! The first pickpocket looks into his jeans . . . shrieks . . . and runs offstage. The winner is handed his prize.

6.

The King's Royal Papers

CAST: King, courtiers, queen, prince, etc.

SCENE: Throne room.

ACTION: The king is on his throne. He beckons to a herald and whispers something. The herald announces, "The king demands his royal papers!" A courtier runs in with a sheaf of papers. The king tosses them aside. The herald makes the announcement again. The queen runs in with newspapers. The king tosses these aside too. Another announcement is made. The king is getting more and more agitated. The herald announces with desperation. People run in with magazines, letters, books, etc. None of this seems to be what the king means by "royal papers."

ENDING: The court jester (or the tiny prince) comes in and presents the king with . . . a roll of toilet paper. The king grabs his sword, knights the jester, and runs off.

Variant

A boss in his office wants his "important papers."

The Elevator

CAST: Elevator operator, any number of passengers.

SCENE: Inside a department store elevator.

ACTION: An elevator operator intones "Ground Floor" and opens the door. A passenger gets on and begins to jiggle slightly as the elevator rises. The elevator operator announces each floor: "First Floor, Women's Lingerie." She opens the door and another passenger gets on and begins to jiggle too. Continue up through as many floors as you need to get your whole group onto the elevator. "Second Floor, Men's Clothing"; "Sixth Floor, Kitchenware"; etc. As the elevator rises higher and higher, the passengers jiggle more and more.

ENDING: The elevator stops. The operator calls "Top Floor, Last Stop." Everyone starts to jiggle like mad. "Bathrooms . . . !" Everyone rushes off the elevator and races offstage toward the bathrooms. The elevator operator shakes her head in disbelief. Suddenly she looks funny and she, too, begins to jiggle. The operator shouts, "Me, too!" and rushes off after them.

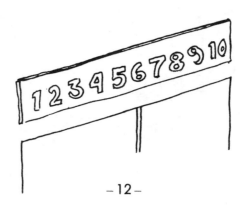

8.

Presents for the Teacher

CAST: Teacher, students.

SCENE: Classroom.

ACTION: Children come into the class with presents for the teacher. The teacher says, "Welcome to the first day of school. Oh, I see you've brought presents for the teacher." The first child brings a present and the teacher unwraps it. It is stationery. Teacher: "I'll bet your parents own the stationery store downtown." The student says, "Wow! How did you guess?" Second student brings up a basket of apples. Teacher: "I'll bet your parents run the fruitstand on the edge of town." Student: "That's right!" The baker's child can bring rolls, the candymaker's child brings candy, etc.

ENDING: The last package is wrapped crudely. Yellow liquid is leaking from the bottom of the package. The teacher tastes the liquid with her finger and smiles. "Oh . . . orange pop. I'll bet *your* family runs the pop bottling factory." Kid: "Nope. My dad's the dogcatcher. That's a puppy."

9.

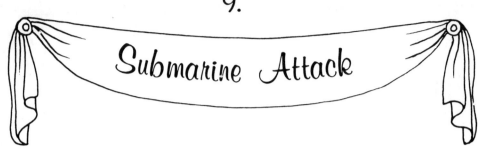

Submarine Attack

CAST: Submarine captain and crew.

SCENE: A submarine.

ACTION: Crew is seated in line, one behind the other. The gunner is last in line. The gunner passes word up to the front: "Can I fire now?" Each sailor passes the question to the person in front until it reaches the captain. The captain sends back the message, "No. Not yet." Repeat this chain message several times, putting lots of tension into the moment.

ENDING: The captain finally passes the order down the line: "Okay. FIRE!" The gunner fires. The entire crew turns to watch the torpedo go. Then they break into a cheer and begin to sing, "We sunk a rowboat! We sunk a rowboat!"

10.

The Airplane Crash

CAST: Pilot, stewardess, passengers.

SCENE: An airplane in flight.

ACTION: The stewardess welcomes the passengers to the plane. "Welcome aboard Flight 121, the Camp Huston Special. Please fasten your seatbelts for take-off." The passengers all buckle up. They lean back in synchronized motion as the plane takes off. All make the "vrooom" noise of engines as they lift off. The plane settles into a normal flight pattern and all return to upright positions in their seats.

The stewardess leaves the stage and her voice is now heard as if on an intercom. She can talk through a megaphone made from a rolled-up newspaper if you don't have a microphone to use. The stewardess announces that the left wing is on fire. The passengers all lean to the left and look out. "I'm sorry to trouble you passengers, but it appears our RIGHT wing is now on fire." They all lean and look out the right window in terror. "Please don't be alarmed, but that speck you see falling toward the ground is our co-pilot bailing out." Everyone gasps in horror. "Now promise you won't panic. That second speck you see falling from the plane appears to be our pilot bailing out." Everyone is now about to panic.

ENDING: "Thank you for flying Air Camp Huston. I've enjoyed serving you. That last person you see bailing out is your stewardess. Thank God this is a recording."

Everyone jumps up and panics off stage screaming.

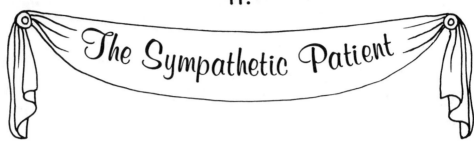

The Sympathetic Patient

CAST: Receptionist in doctor's office, patient who catches all ills, other patients, doctor.

SCENE: Doctor's waiting room.

ACTION: Patient sits in waiting room reading a magazine. Another patient enters, tells the receptionist he has the hives, and scratches all over. The first patient begins to scratch too. The doctor sticks his head out of his office and calls, "Next." The scratching patient goes in to see the doctor. Another patient comes onstage. This one tells the nurse he has a horrid headache. Patient number one, who is still scratching the hives he caught from the second patient, now gets a splitting headache as well. Add as many patients as you like. Each time someone enters, the waiting patient catches whatever they have. Soon he has a headache, stomach ache, sore foot, hives, etc.

ENDING: A patient enters who is very pregnant. The patient who catches everything screams, "NO, NOT THAT!" and runs off the stage.

Variant

Sometimes this is performed with the examining doctor curing everyone by taking on their diseases. As he examines them he suddenly acquires their hives, headache, etc., and they are as suddenly cured. The skit ends as the pregnant woman comes on stage and the doctor rushes off screaming, "Anything but THAT!"

12.

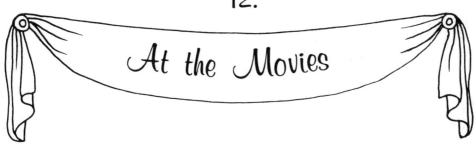

At the Movies

CAST: A boyfriend and girlfriend. Several moviegoers.

SCENE: The movie theater.

ACTION: A row of people are watching the movie. A couple sits at one end. The girl asks for popcorn. The boy passes money down the row for someone to go buy it. The end person goes out and returns with the popcorn. It's best to use imaginary food rather than real food, since everyone has to share it. As the popcorn is passed back down the aisle to the girl, everyone takes a handful. When it reaches her the box is empty. She turns the box upside down and shows it to the audience in disgust. The boyfriend orders her a Coke. The same routine is followed. Again, everyone takes a drink as it passes down the line and it reaches the girlfriend empty. She orders candy with the same result.

ENDING: The girl orders chewing gum. As it passes down the line everyone chews it for awhile and then passes it on. When it reaches the girl she throws all her empty containers at her boyfriend and stalks out shouting, "THAT DOES IT!"

13.

The Naughty Student

CAST: Teacher, naughty student, other students.

SCENE: A classroom.

ACTION: A teacher is trying to control a roomful of kids. One kid keeps throwing spitballs. The teacher can't tell who is doing this. Every time a spitball flies the teacher takes a student offstage and spanks him. The audience hears the whacking offstage. The teacher comes back dusting his hands together as if to say, "I sure took care of that!" and the culprit stays offstage. Repeat this until all but the one truly naughty kid have been taken out and spanked.

ENDING: The naughty kid shoots another spitball, and like the resf, is dragged offstage by the teacher. There is a sound of spanking again. Then the naughty student comes back onstage alone, dusting her hands together in the same proud way the teacher had used.

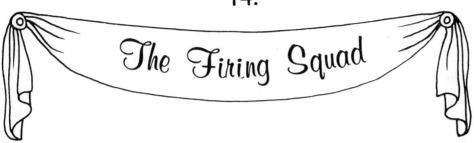

The Firing Squad

CAST: Soldiers, and a captain who gives orders. Prisoners for execution.

SCENE: A firing squad execution wall. Prisoners in a cell at one side nervously watch the action and are brought out one by one.

ACTION: The firing squad aims rifles at a prisoner. The captain calls, "Ready . . . Aim . . . ." The prisoner shouts, "*Tornado!*" The soldiers all run for cover and the prisoner escapes. A second prisoner is brought out. "Ready . . . Aim . . . ." The prisoner calls out, "*Earthquake!*" Everyone runs for cover and the prisoner escapes. Repeat this using as many natural disasters as you like: flood, landslide, etc.

ENDING: The last prisoner is brought out. The same sequence is used. "Ready . . . Aim . . . ." This prisoner thinks quickly, having seen the others escape, and yells out, "*Fire!*"
   The soldiers do.

15.

The Mysterious Flying Object

CAST: Person with a stiff neck, as many passersby as you like.

ACTION: One person walks onstage with head tilted up at an awkward angle, stops, and stares up into the sky. The position of this person's head should not change during the entire skit. One by one others walk on stage, notice this staring person, and look up to see what she is looking at. All comment to one another: "Do you see it?" "There it goes!" "I think I saw it just then!" etc. They clearly believe something is up there and talk excitedly about the mysterious flying object in the sky.

ENDING: The last person to come onstage asks the person on the end of the line what he is looking at. That person asks the next person, "Do you know what we're looking at?" "No. I thought you did." He asks the next person in line. "Do you know what we're looking at?" The question passes down the line in this way, finally reaching the first person. She is still staring up into the sky and has taken no notice of the people behind her. She is tapped on the shoulder. "Pardon me . . . but what is it we're looking at?" The first person turns with her head still cocked awkwardly.

    "Oh, hi. I didn't see you all there. I'm afraid I've got a stiff neck today."

16.

The Candy Contest

CAST: Candy store owner, kids eating candy.

SCENE: A candy store. Table with jars of candy.

ACTION: Kids come into store and start buying candy. One asks for a dozen licorice sticks, and eats them all at once. Another asks for twenty gumdrops and gobbles them up. A third buys fifteen candycanes and crunches them up. You will have to mime this massive eating binge. They stuff themselves with an assortment of candy until all begin to look ill and hold their stomachs.

ENDING: The leader of the candy-eating gang says, "We've gotta go now." Candy store owner: "Why is that?" "Oh, we're on our way to a candy-eating contest. We just came in to practice."

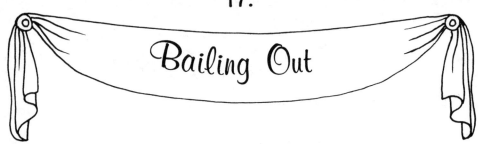

17.

Bailing Out

CAST: A Boy Scout, a priest, the Smartest-Man-in-the-World, and an airplane pilot. Add more characters if needed.

SCENE: A crashing airplane.

ACTION: The group is flying in an airplane. The Smartest-Man-in-the-World starts showing off his knowledge, telling the passengers all about the airplane, all about the country they are flying over, etc. He keeps telling them that he is the Smartest-Man-in-the-World. Make it clear through the conversation that one of the passengers is a priest and one is a Boy Scout (Girl Scout, Camp Huston camper, etc.). After the actors have had time to improvise enough to establish their characters, the pilot announces that the plane is going to crash. "I'm sorry, folks, but the plane is going to crash. You'll all have to bail out. I'm afraid there aren't enough parachutes for everyone on board. But I've got mine! Good luck." He jumps out and disappears offstage in free fall.

The Smartest-Man-in-the-World says, "Well, the Smartest-Man-in-the-World isn't about to get caught without a parachute . . . I've got MINE!" He freefalls offstage. The priest and the Boy Scout are left. The priest offers to let the Boy Scout take the final parachute.

ENDING: The Boy Scout says, "Thanks, but it's no problem. I've got a parachute. The Smartest-Man-in-the-World took my backpack!" The priest and the Boy Scout jump.

18.

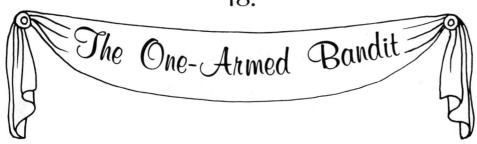

The One-Armed Bandit

CAST: "One-armed bandit" slot machine, any number of players. The "one-armed bandit" player might wear a paper box or paper bag costume with dials and lights drawn on. The machine should stand with one arm bent at the elbow, the hand pointing up. This arm is pulled down to activate the machine.

SCENE: A pinball arcade.

ACTION: A player enters and puts a coin in the "one-armed bandit." The object is to outdraw the machine with a pistol. The player then takes five paces away from the machine, whirls, and fires on the count of five. The machine easily wins and shoots the player. A series of players enter and are defeated by the machine.

ENDING: A fast-draw expert enters and tells the audience how good he is. He puts in a quarter and outshoots the machine, gloats over this, and puts in another quarter. This time the machine refuses to draw. The fast-draw expert gloats again and turns to go. The machine draws and plugs the fast-draw expert in the back, blows on its pistol, and turns into an innocent machine again.

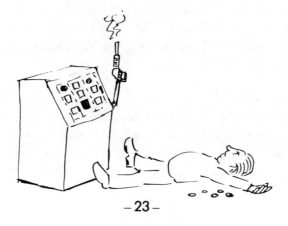

19.

Johnny Got Run Over by a Bus:

Shooting the Movie

CAST: Movie director, cameraman, actors, bus, ambulance.

SCENE: A movie set.

ACTION: A director is trying to film a scene. Cameraman shoots the action while the actors play it. Johnny is playing ball, runs into the street and is run over by a bus. A group of kids chugging along together form the bus. An ambulance comes onstage and carries Johnny off. The ambulance is played by another group of kids. These roles may all be double-cast, and everyone must be running around hard trying to bring this off. The director calls, "Cut" and says to do it over again — only this time make it sadder. The players repeat the action making everything exaggeratedly sad. The director calls, "Cut. Do it over. Make it faster this time." The director keeps asking for them to do the scene over until everyone is exasperated. Meanwhile the cameraman is filming away madly and making a big deal of the filming.

ENDING: The director yells, "Cut. That's just what I wanted! You can all go home!" The cameraman shouts, "Stop!" and whispers to the director, "Maybe we ought to shoot it just once more." Director: "Why?" Cameraman: "I forgot to put film in the camera."
Everyone chases the cameraman off the stage.

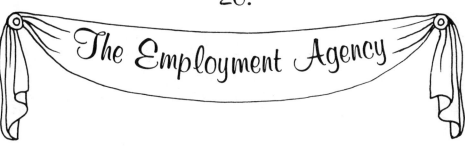

The Employment Agency

CAST: Secretary, personnel director.

SCENE: An employment agency.

ACTION: Applicants arrive looking for a job. They are received by the secretary, who takes their names. They are famous characters: Cinderella, Little Red Riding Hood, the Big Bad Wolf, etc. The personnel director interviews each. They tell him their qualifications for the jobs they want. Let each character decide what job to apply for and make up their qualifications. For example, Little Red Riding Hood might be applying for pizza delivery, but the personnel director could discover through questioning that she didn't do so well on her last delivery job. The Big Bad Wolf might apply to be a hog farmer, and so on.

ENDING: The personnel director tells the applicants he can't place them in the jobs they want, but asks them to wait. He makes a phone call: "Mr. Disney? I think I've got just what you need here. Yes. I'll send them right over!"

21.

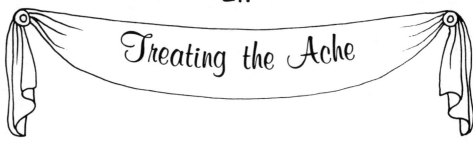

Treating the Ache

CAST: Nurse, patients.

SCENE: Doctor's office.

ACTION: A patient is waiting to see the doctor. Another patient complains of a sore toe. Goes in. Comes back out with toe bandaged. First patient asks, "What happened?" Second patient explains, "My toe ached so the doctor cut it off!" Another patient goes in complaining of a sore hand, and comes back out with a bandaged hand. She explains, "My hand ached so the doctor cut it off." Another has an earache, and another a toothache, with the same results. The first patient is becoming more and more alarmed.

ENDING: When the nurse finally calls the waiting patient, he jumps up and starts to run out of the waiting room. The nurse calls after him, "Wait . . . what's the matter?"
　　　　　Patient: "You don't understand, nurse. I've got a HEADACHE!"

22.

The Biggest Liars in Texas

CAST: Several fishermen, the game warden.

SCENE: A river bank.

ACTION: Several fishermen come in, one at a time, and eagerly start telling a person they meet onstage about all of the fish they have caught. He listens with interest and asks questions, "Is that so? You mean you caught forty-five perch just today? Hmmmm." He could take notes on their big catches and write down their names, feigning interest.

ENDING: After the last fisherman has arrived and told another big fish story, the person who has been listening to all of this and taking notes says, "Do you know who I am? I'm the GAME WARDEN." The fishermen look panicky, except for the first fisherman. He doesn't even bat an eye, just turns and drawls, "Glad to meet you, Game Warden. I guess you don't know who we are. We're the BIGGEST LIARS IN TEXAS!" All repeat with relief, "Yeah, the BIGGEST LIARS IN TEXAS!" and they rush off the stage. Game Warden looks after them shaking his head in disbelief.

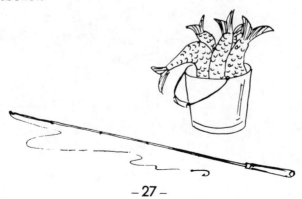

23.

Goodbye in Any Language

CAST: Many speakers of foreign languages, one leader.

ACTION: Cast member comes onstage and greets leader, "Hi, how are you?" They talk for awhile. Just invent some dialogue. Make it humorous if you like, but keep it brief. When the actor turns to go he calls out, "*Hasta Luego!*" Leader: "What does that mean?" "Oh, that means 'goodbye' in Spanish." The person leaves. Other cast members come onstage one at a time, chat briefly and then leave saying goodbye in a foreign language. (*Buon giorno,* Italian; *Au revoir,* French; *Sayonara,* Japanese; *Dosvidanya,* Russian; etc.).

ENDING: Last cast member comes on, chats with the leader, and leaves calling, "Atom Bomb." "And what does *that* mean?" asks the leader. "That means 'goodbye' in *any* language!"

Igor Kill

CAST: A mad scientist, victims, Igor. Igor should be a Frankenstein monster-like creation. You can make him really huge by putting one performer on the shoulders of another and wrapping a sheet around the shoulders of the top performer. It should reach to the ground and cover both actors.

SCENE: Mad scientist's laboratory.

ACTION: A mad scientist introduces his creation, "Igor." Igor has been trained to eliminate the scientist's enemies on command. An enemy enters and the scientist utters, "IGOR KILL!" Igor destroys the enemy. Repeat this several times with various enemies. Let Igor stagger about, knocking over robbers, police, other monsters. Invent characters to expand the skit.

ENDING: The scientist explains to the audience that Igor never fails to kill when given the command, "IGOR KILL!" This time there is no enemy in sight to kill, so Igor kills . . . the scientist!

25.

Hot News

CAST: Reporters, newspaper editor.

SCENE: A newspaper office.

ACTION: In an office reporters are busily typing stories. The boss enters and tells them she wants only "hot news" for this paper. If they can't bring her "hot news" they will be fired. A reporter leaves, saying he's going to look for a story. Soon the reporter rushes back. "Hot news! Hot news! Have I got a story!" Boss: "What is it?" Reporter: "A barn burned down in Redmond yesterday!" Boss: "Yesterday! That's not hot news! That's *old* news. You're fired!" A second reporter leaves to look for a story and returns shouting, "Hot news! Hot news!" Boss: "What is it?" Reporter: "There was a robbery in Bellevue last night!" Boss: "Last night! That's not hot news! You're fired!" A third reporter tells of a murder this morning, with the same result. Add as many reporters as you like.

ENDING: The last reporter, who has been watching all this carefully, leaves and soon rushes back in. "Hot news! Hot news!" Boss: "What *is* it?" Reporter: "The building across the street just blew up!" Pause. There is a loud explosion offstage. Everyone does a doubletake at the reporter who responds with an "Ooops!" and runs offstage. All can collapse in desperation *or* chase the reporter offstage.

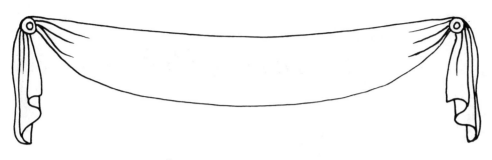

Skits Using Word Play

These skits all depend on the double meanings of words. The audience thinks one thing is intended, but at the end of the skit another meaning is revealed. These skits are often derived from jokes, although some, such as "The Frogs Go Whee!", must have originated as camp skits. Try making up your own humorous skit, using a word which has two meanings.

The Viper is Coming

CAST: A window wiper, the boss, secretaries, assistants, etc.

SCENE: An office.

ACTION: The boss is relaxing with his feet on his desk when his secretary rushes in excitedly. "I just had a phone call. The Viper is coming!" The boss is upset: "Oh, no! The VIPER is coming!" Another person rushes in: "Have you heard? The VIPER is coming!" One after another all rush in with the terrifying news that "The Viper" is coming. Everyone is in a state of panic.

ENDING: A person in blue jeans with a cloth hanging out of his back pocket, carrying a squeegee and sponge, enters and announces "I'm the vindow viper. I've come to vipe your vindows. Vere do I start?"

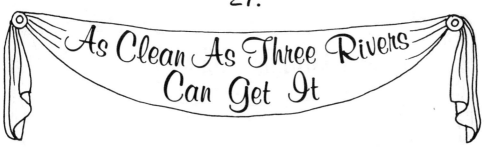

27.

As Clean As Three Rivers Can Get It

CAST: An oldtimer, a dog, hungry campers with plates around campfire. You may want to pin fake ears and a tail on the "dog."

SCENE: Campfire in the wilds.

ACTION: An oldtimer is cooking. A hungry camper enters and picks up a plate. "Good grief. This plate is filthy!" The camper raises a fuss about the dirty state of the plate. The oldtimer vows that the plate is "as clean as Three Rivers can get it." One by one other campers enter and repeat this complaint. Each time, the oldtimer says, "I don't know what you're complaining about. That plate is as clean as Three Rivers can get it." When all are around the campfire the oldtimer serves the meal and they gobble it up, then pass their plates and utensils back to the oldtimer.

ENDING: The oldtimer spreads the plates and utensils out on the ground and calls offstage, "Here, Three Rivers, come see how clean you can get 'em this time." A dog lumbers on stage and starts licking the plates.

Variant

As Clean As Ocean Can Get It. This skit can be set at a seaside restaurant. The cook keeps telling customers that the plates are "as clean as ocean can get them." After the meal "ocean" is called. "Ocean" is the cook's pet dog.

Minnie Muscles

CAST: Exercising boys. A curvaceous girl.

SCENE: A gym.

ACTION: The stage is full of boys exercising madly. They could be jump-
          ing rope, lifting weights, etc. A visitor enters and asks the first
          boy he meets why he is exercising so hard. The boy replies that
          he wants "many muscles." The visitor asks each boy in turn this
          same question and all answer the same way. "Many muscles"
          should be pronounced tightly as "miny muscles."

ENDING: A curvaceous girl walks on stage. Visitor asks, "Who are you?"
          Girl: "Oh, hi. I'm Minnie Muscles!" All boys follow her
          quickly offstage.

Picking Up Pebbles

CAST: Judge, policemen, offenders, girl, reporter.

SCENE: Courtroom.

ACTION: Two policemen drag an offender before the judge. Judge: "And what is this man accused of?" Policeman: "He was caught on the beach trying to pick up pebbles." Judge: "That's disgraceful! Give that man thirty days in jail." A reporter is covering the story. He is aghast and talks to the audience: "That's absurd. He gave that man thirty days in jail just for picking up pebbles on the beach!" A second man is brought in with the same offense. He is given the same sentence. The reporter becomes increasingly upset as more defendants are brought in with the same charge.

ENDING: A girl in a bathing suit walks on stage. All do a double take and stare at her. The reporter rushes up. "Pardon me, Miss, but who are YOU?"

Girl: "Oh, I've just come from the beach. They call me PEBBLES."

Variant

Kids are punished for throwing "Pebbles" in the lake.

The Frogs Go Whee!

CAST: Little frogs, a frog leader.

SCENE: A swamp.

ACTION: A frog leader is directing a frog chorus. They can be singing any song you all know — just sing it in "ribbits." One by one the little frogs come up and tug on the frog leader saying, "I wanna go WEE! I wanna go WEE!" The frog leader whispers, "Not NOW!" and sends each back to its place in the chorus. Repeat this until each little frog has asked to go "wee" and the leader is at wits' end trying to hold the chorus together.

ENDING: At last the leader gives up. "ALL RIGHT. You can all go wee now!" As the leader turns away, the little frogs all jump into the air together and yell "WHEEEEE!"

Variant

The Little One Goes Whee. The characters here can be a group of campers with a leader. The littlest camper repeatedly asks the camper next to her if she can go "wee." The message is passed up the line each time to the leader, who passes back the answer, "No, not YET." At last the answer is "Yes, now you can go wee." The littlest camper on the end leaps into the air: "WHEEE!"

"Shut Up" and Her Dog "Trouble"

CAST: "Shut Up," her dog "Trouble," teachers, school secretary, vice-principal, principal.

SCENE: A school.

ACTION: Shut Up skips onstage with her dog Trouble. She introduces herself to the audience: "Hi, my name is Shut Up. Don't laugh. That's really my name. And this is my dog. Her name is Trouble." While Shut Up is talking, Trouble runs off. Shut Up calls Trouble but can't get her to return. She is upset about losing Trouble but has to go on to school. She tells the audience that today is her first day at the new school.

At school the teacher asks what her name is. She answers, "Shut Up." The teacher keeps asking and getting the same answer so she sends Shut Up to the principal's office. The secretary asks her name and is told, "Shut Up." The vice-principal is called. You can add more teachers or vice-principals if you want.

ENDING: At last the principal comes and demands, "What is your name, young lady?"
"Shut Up!"
"Shut Up is it? Are you looking for TROUBLE?"
"I sure am! Have you seen her?"

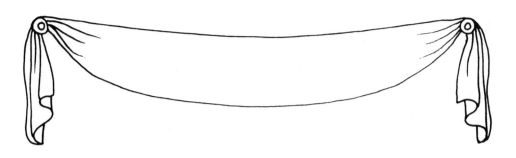

Tricking the Dupe

A popular form of skit is one which pokes fun at authorities — teachers, counselors, principals, and the like. A person who does not realize he is being fooled is called a "dupe." The skits in this section are all designed to play a trick on such an unsuspecting member of the audience.

It is important to be careful in your choice of a dupe. Always choose someone with a good sense of humor. Choose someone who will find the trick funny and go along with the joke. Never use the "dupe" skits as a way to actually ridicule someone. They should just be used to have fun with the people you like best. It is a good idea to plan in advance exactly who you will call to the stage as your dupe. Have a back-up dupe in mind, in case the person you hoped to use can't be located when your skit goes onstage, or catches on and refuses to be "duped."

Similar to "dupe" skits are camp "biffs" — short bits that poke fun at a counselor. These are acted out on regular campfire nights, not at skit night. For example, a camper pretends to present a flower to a counselor, makes a great speech about it, then dumps a sack of flour on her head and waters it!

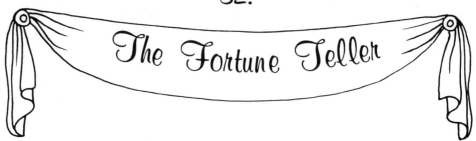

32.

The Fortune Teller

CAST: Fortune teller, assistant, fortune seekers planted in the audience, announcer.

ACTION: A fortune teller comes on and sits cross-legged on stage. The announcer explains that the swami can tell fortunes, and asks for volunteers from the audience. Several members of the skit-performing group are "planted" in the audience. The fortune teller's assistant picks one of these to come onstage. The fortune teller asks for a shoe from the volunteer. The fortune teller sniffs the shoe, examines it, and says she foresees great luck in this person's future. As the volunteer starts to leave the stage, she bends over and finds a four-leaf clover: "See, my luck has started already!" A second volunteer is brought up. The fortune teller consults his shoe and predicts treasure in the future. This volunteer finds a quarter on the stage! Repeat this with as many fortunes as you like.

ENDING: The accomplice now picks someone who is not in on the skit and brings him forward to have his fortune told. The fortune teller asks for a shoe . . . sniffs it, says, "I foresee great travels in your future," and throws the shoe as far as she can!

33.

The Candy Store

CAST: Candy store owner, customers

SCENE: A candy store

ACTION: A candy store owner enters carrying a long pole. The owner asks two individuals from the audience to come up and hold the pole. The owner drapes a scarf over the pole and explains to the audience that this is a candy store. One by one, customers come up and ask for certain kinds of candy. The owner doesn't have any of them. "Sorry, no gumdrops today." "Nope, I don't have any M & M's," etc.

ENDING: The frustrated customers all gang up on the candy store owner. "You don't have gumdrops, you don't have candy canes, you don't have M & M's. What kind of candy store *is* this?" Candy store owner replies, "Well, I don't have any of those candies. But I *do* have two suckers on a stick!" Pulls scarf off pole and indicates two audience members foolishly holding up the stick.

The Squirrel's Harvest

CAST: Announcer and squirrels. Ears can be pinned on, a tail added, and face make-up used. Or you can just improvise the motions of squirrels.

ACTION: The announcer asks the audience to cooperate with the squirrels' harvest. The squirrels race into the audience and bring onto the stage certain people who are known for their crazy behavior. These are gathered into a group in center stage.

ENDING: The announcer says that the title of the skit will now be announced: "The Gathering of the Nuts!"

Fish Market Calling

CAST: Fish market manager, Joe the fisherman, assistants.

SCENE: Fish market, fishing dock, telephone line between. The fish market manager and Joe each hold one end of a long line. A clothesline or fishing line will do.

ACTION: The fish market manager dials Joe the fisherman and asks if he has any fresh trout today. Joe pretends not to be able to hear and says the line is bad. The assistants select a volunteer from the audience to help hold up the line. The fishmarket manager calls again, but Joe still can't hear. The assistants bring someone else to help hold the line. Repeat this until you have several dupes standing on stage holding up the line.

ENDING: Joe the fisherman finally hears the question correctly and answers, "Sorry, I don't have any trout today. But I do have a whole line full of SUCKERS!" Joe raises the line showing off the volunteers who are foolishly holding it up.

36.

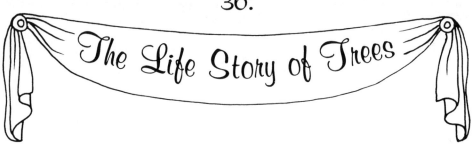

The Life Story of Trees

CAST: Narrator, many people to play the part of trees.

SCENE: A forest.

ACTION: The narrator announces that this is the story of the life of trees. The "trees" act out the story as the narrator talks. "In the summer the trees lift their branches to the sky and sway in the breezes." All trees lift their arms and sway. "But in the autumn the leaves fall to the ground." Pantomime falling leaves. "The sap runs down into the roots and trees droop their branches and die down." Trees droop to the floor. "But in the spring the sap runs up again into the trees' branches. The trees lift their branches and sway in the breeze." Trees all straighten up and sway again.

After you have acted out this "life cycle" once, the narrator picks a dupe from the audience to come onstage. This must be someone who can take a joke. Ask the dupe to run through the forest while you tell the rest of the story. Repeat the life cycle of the trees, passing through all of the seasons and mentioning the sap a lot.

ENDING: When you have gone through the whole year once or twice, stop at winter and say, "Winter came and the trees died down . . . ." All the trees are now slumped over on stage. The narrator pauses and says pointedly, "But the SAP is still running." Point out the dupe still running among the trees.

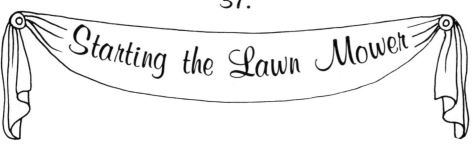

Starting the Lawn Mower

CAST: Lawn mower, owner, people to help start the lawn mower.

SCENE: A backyard.

ACTION: One person huddles over pantomiming a lawn mower. This "mower" rumbles and shakes as each person tries to start it, then sputters and dies. The gardener tries to start it and fails. Other skit members try their luck, No one can get it started.

ENDING: The gardener selects a dupe from the audience to try to start the machine. It starts right up and begins to chug away. The gardener explains to the audience, "All it took was a bigger JERK."

38.

The Echo

CAST: A tour guide, tourists, assistants hidden to provide echo.

SCENE: The site of a remarkable echo.

ACTION: The tour guide lectures to the tourists and audience about the remarkable natural echo in this spot. A tourist is invited to come and try it out. This person calls out something like "Helloooo Theeeeer . . . ." The echo repeats it. The tourist is impressed. Another tourist tries it. Again the echo comes back loud and clear. Repeat this several times.

ENDING: Finally, the last tourist calls out something to tease a teacher, counselor, or other "dupe": "Jay Powers is a handsome brute!" The echo answers back: "You're craaazy . . . !"

Variant

The most common form of this skit seems to be for the echo to answer at the end "Baloooooney!"

The Human Bonfire

CAST: Bonfire builders, leader.

SCENE: A campfire.

ACTION: A leader begins to explain how to lay a fire. The leader decides to use members of the audience to represent various kinds of wood. The bonfire builders bring up volunteers. Some dupes are bunched in the middle as tinder. Others are placed for kindling. The big "logs" are stacked on top of each other in increasingly larger sizes.

ENDING: The leader says the fire is now ready to light and strikes a match. Several accomplices cry out, "Good grief! It's ON FIRE!" and dash buckets of water on the "bonfire."

NOTE: Make sure you clear this with the person in charge beforehand as some of the dupes will get very wet. Or you could fill the bucket with confetti just to make them think it is water.

40.

The Coffee Shop Table

CAST: Waitress, cook, head waiter, hostess, diners, announcer.

SCENE: A restaurant.

ACTION: An announcer comes on stage and asks for an audience member to help with the skit. This dupe is told to get down on hands and knees. The back of this person is then used as a table during the skit. The hostess shows the diners to their seats. The waitress comes and places menus on the "table" and takes the orders. The waitress brings plastic plates, glasses of water, cups, etc., and places them on the dupe's back. The diners start an argument about the food. The head waiter is called; then the cook is called. The argument climaxes with much shouting.

ENDING: The diners get up and stalk out of the restaurant. The cook, head waiter, and waitress turn and stalk back into the kitchen. The hostess shrugs and leaves too. The "table" is left there with glasses of water on its back. The audience now waits to see how the dupe will get out of this predicament.

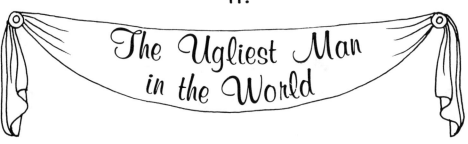

The Ugliest Man in the World

CAST: The Ugliest Man in the World, bystanders, carnival barker.

SCENE: Sideshow.

ACTION: Carnival barker calls for people to step right up and see the Ugliest Man in the World. The barker warns that anyone who looks in the face of the Ugliest Man in the World will die. The Ugliest Man has his head down and his hat pulled down. One by one bystanders come up and pay to see the Ugliest Man. Each dares to look into his face. Each falls dead.

ENDING: The carnival barker asks a dupe from the audience to come up and have a look. When this dupe looks into the face of the Ugliest Man in the World, the Ugliest Man shrieks and falls over dead!

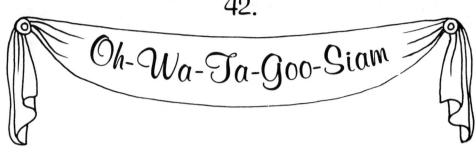

Oh-Wa-Ta-Goo-Siam

CAST: Guru in turban. Assistants to bring on dupes from audience.

SCENE: Guru is conducting an enlightenment session.

ACTION: Members of audience are solicited to take part in the session. They are told that they should repeat the magic phrase after the guru. Whenever this phrase brings about enlightenment for the chanter, that chanter may get up and return to the audience. In other words, as they catch on they get up and go back to their seats. All sit cross-legged on the floor and follow the guru. The guru carries on a great deal, raising his arms to the sky as he chants, "Oh . . . Wa . . . Ta . . . Goo . . . Siam . . . ." All chant with him. Keep this up for a long while.

ENDING: Eventually everyone catches on to the fact that they are really saying, "Oh, what a goose I am."

NOTE: This will work only with fairly young dupes who haven't heard it before.

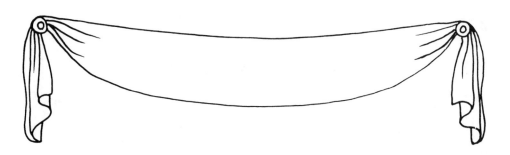

Grossies

A few of the skits kids told me about are gross. Neverthe-less, several kids mentioned these skits, giving the im-pression that they are fairly popular. Or perhaps they are just so gross that everybody remembers them. I'm calling them "Grossies" and am giving you a sample here. I col-lected a few more, but they were just *too* gross to even consider actually performing, unless you want the entire audience to vomit right then and there. Here are a few which seem pretty disgusting, but stop just short of being barfable. These skits may be so popular because they provide a way to get by with stuff that adults normally would put a halt to.

43.

The Toothbrushers

CAST: As many toothbrushing kids as you like.

ACTION: A row of kids are getting ready to brush their teeth. They have only one cup of water to use. The first brusher pours water into the cup. The cup must be opaque so the audience can't see through it, but they must see the water being poured into it. The first brusher pretends to brush her teeth with the water, then gargles and pretends to spit it back into the cup. Actually she swallows the water, but the audience must not know that the cup is now empty. She hands the cup to the second brusher who pretends to brush and gargle with the same water and then spit it back into the cup. Pass this action down the line of tooth brushers. It gets more gross as it goes.

ENDING: The last person in line has been holding a mouthful of water during the entire skit. Be sure to choose someone for this job who can keep a straight face throughout the skit. After she pretends to brush, she actually spits her mouthful of water into the cup. This time hold the cup far enough away from the mouth to make sure the audience sees that a mouthful of water is really being spit into the cup. If done properly this should gross them out.

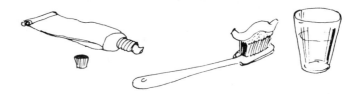

44.

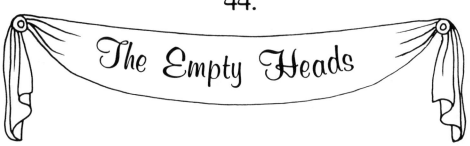

The Empty Heads

CAST: Many empty-headed participants, announcer.

ACTION: The participants are lined up. The announcer explains that these remarkable people all have empty heads. To demonstrate this, the first person in line takes a huge drink of water from a glass. His cheeks bulge out with the water. He then pretends to spit the water in the ear of the next person in line. Actually he just lets the air out of his cheeks, only pretending to have a mouth full of water. As the "water" enters her ear, the second person balloons her cheeks to make it look like they are filling with water. Practice this. It must look as if the second person's mouth is filling up as the first person's mouth empties. Keep passing the "water" down the line until it reaches the last person.

ENDING: The last person in line receives the "water" in his ear, puffs up his cheeks, and spits the water into a glass! This time it is real water, for the last person had a mouthful of water during the entire skit without letting anyone know.

Green Hair

CAST: Green-haired kids, friend.

ACTION: Kid comes on stage with green hair. A friend asks, "How did your hair get green?" First kid replies, "I walked under a ladder and green paint fell on my head." A second green-haired kid comes on stage. "How did your hair get green?" "My mother was spray-painting a chair and I walked past." Use as many green-haired kids as you like, with similar excuses. You can use green food coloring or green hairspray to color the hair. Be sure to wash your hair immediately afterwards.

ENDING: The last green-haired kid comes on stage. The friend asks, "How did *your* hair get so green?" Kid wipes nose with upward movement as if smearing snot up onto bangs and hair. "Gee. I don't know."

46.

The Super Duper Rainbow-Flavored Bubble Gum

CAST: A bubblegum chewer, several passersby, and a dog.

SCENE: A city street, a park bench.

ACTION: A gum chewer skips on stage happily chewing gum. The gum chewer sits down on a park bench, takes out the gum, and raves about the wonders of this gum. It is the best ever found . . . rainbow-colored . . . multi-flavored . . . etc. The gum chewer sticks the gum on the bench while talking. Someone calls from offstage and the chewer runs off, forgetting the gum. A passerby comes along and sees the gum. This person picks it up, examines it, chews it awhile, and puts it back. Several people come by, one by one, and each does something gross to the gum. They spit on the gum . . . use it to stick broken glasses together while reading . . . play with it like silly putty . . . etc. Finally a dog comes by and pees on the gum.

ENDING: The gum chewer comes running back to retrieve the forgotten wad of gum. Chewer pops it into the mouth, and exclaims again over this incredible many-flavored gum!

The Fly

CAST: Several people passing by.

SCENE: A public place with a table or bench.

ACTION: Someone is reading at a bench. A fly begins buzzing around, and is eventually swatted and left lying on the tabletop. A passerby comes along, sees the dead fly, and fools with it, pulling off the wings. The passerby should talk about what he is doing so the audience knows he pulled off the wings as this is all too small to actually be seen. Another person comes by and pulls the feet off the fly. Another comes along and pulls off the head, etc.

ENDING: A last passerby comes along, sees the footless, wingless, headless body of the fly and exclaims, "Oh, goody! A RAISIN!" and pops it into the mouth.

48.

Got the Beat

CAST: Series of finger-snapping kids.

SCENE: City street.

ACTION: First kid comes onstage snapping fingers and rapping:

> "I got the beat.
> I got the beat.
> I got the beat . . . beat . . . beat . . . ."

Creepy-looking kid is standing on the opposite side of the stage. The finger-snapper crosses stage, gives creepy kid five (slaps hand) and moves to the back of the stage, where he continues to snap fingers and rap under his breath. One by one other actors come on snapping fingers and repeat the high five action with the creepy kid. They can use the same words, or make up a similar chant with the same rhythm.

ENDING: All the actors are lined up across the rear of the stage snapping and chanting. The creepy kid begins to cross stage snapping *his* fingers as if he is trying to shake something from them. He chants to the same beat:

> "I've got a booger
> on my finger
> And I can't
> Get it off."

Kids at rear look at their own fingers (they have just slapped hands with this kid) and race off stage in disgust.

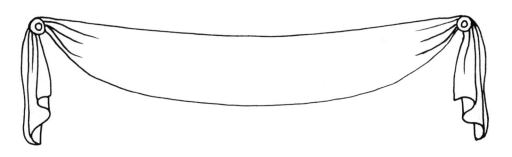

Cumulative Actions

These are stories which start with one motion and keep adding motions until the action becomes totally berserk. Stories with this kind of crazy action are sometimes used as fun activities for groups. One person acts as leader and gets the whole audience to follow in the actions. With a group of comic performers these can also make funny skits. Here are three which can be used for either skits or audience participation.

The Zookeeper and His Animals

CAST: Narrating zookeeper, animals.

SCENE: The zoo.

ACTION: The zookeeper introduces self, bows, and introduces the animals. Each animal must spring into action for a few moments when it is mentioned. "This is Cindy, our somersaulting chimpanzee." "This is Terry, our trumpeting elephant," etc. After all are introduced, the zookeeper begins telling an elaborate story about the antics of the animals in the zoo. Each animal must do its action every time he mentions it. Choose someone for zookeeper who can talk nonstop.

> As the story progresses the keeper begins to mention all of the animals often, requiring them to leap around in a frenzy. The story could be very simple, such as a tale of a little boy who comes to the zoo and feeds peanuts to the elephant, then the chimpanzee, etc. As the story builds, call on the animals more and more frequently. Build the frenzy to a climax and conclude with something that calls on *all* animals at once: "Later that day it was time for the zoo parade. Out came the elephant, the chimpanzee, the bear, the tiger, the lion," etc. Keep repeating things that happen to all the animals until they are worn out: "Suddenly it began to rain on the elephant, the chimpanzee, the bear . . . ." "Then it began to snow on the elephant, the chimpanzee . . . " and so on.

ENDING: At last the animals can take no more. They turn roaring on the zookeeper and chase him offstage. As he flees he concludes, "And the animals turned on their keeper and chased him out of the zoo. The end!"

50.

The Sympathetic Mourners

CAST: Storyteller, many mourners.

ACTION: Mourners are lined up in a row, with the storyteller at one end. The storyteller begins telling about a death. "McGinty is dead." The first mourner asks, "How did he die?" Teller: "With his left arm held high." Holds left arm high to demonstrate. The first mourner turns to the next in line. "McGinty is dead." The next mourner asks, "How did he die?" "With his left arm held high." This passes down the line until all mourners have their left arms in air. The last person repeats, "With his left arm held high! Oh my, Oh my!" All mourners must keep the left arm held high for the rest of the skit, adding other motions as the skit progresses.

Storyteller repeats his tale and adds another motion. "How did he die?" "With his left arm held high, and one foot in the sky." This is passed down the line too. Then the teller adds, "A-blinking one eye." Or, "With his mouth all awry." Etc. Keep passing down motions until the group is contorted into weird positions.

ENDING: At last, when the first mourner asks, "How did he die?," the storyteller shouts, "A-waving goodbye!" All wave together at audience and hop off stage or collapse.

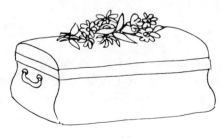

The Button Factory

CAST: Foreman, as many workers as you like, person with sign saying "NEXT DAY."

SCENE: A button factory.

ACTION: The foreman comes in, lines the workers up, and tells them that today is their first day on the job and high productivity is expected. The foreman demonstrates how to turn a little button with the right hand. The workers begin to do this in rhythm. After a while a person crosses the stage carrying a sign saying "NEXT DAY" and calls out, "Next day!" The workers stop their action. The foreman comes onstage again, and says that since they did so well yesterday, today they can turn the button with their right hands and this other button with their left hands. The workers do both in rhythm. Repeat this routine, adding a new movement every day, until each worker is also kicking a lever with the right foot, stamping a button with the left foot, pushing a lever with the right hip, pushing a button with the nose, etc.

ENDING: Person with "NEXT DAY" sign crosses the stage just as the foreman comes on with new instructions. "Next Day!" calls the sign carrier. The workers together shout, "Next day WE QUIT!" and stalk off stage.

Variant

This skit idea can also be used as an audience participation routine. The leader begins a chant which all must follow. Everything must be done in an exact rhythm.

"Hello.
My name is Joe.
I work in a button factory.

"One day
My boss came up to me.
He said, 'Joe, turn this button with your right hand.'
(begin motion)

"Hello.
My name is Joe.
I work in a button factory.

"One day
My boss came up to me.
He said, 'Joe, turn this button with your left hand.'"
(Without stopping right hand motion add left hand motion.
Repeat the chant adding a new motion each time. When every
conceivable part of the body is in motion end with:

"One day
My boss came up to me.
He said . . .
I said, 'I QUIT!'"

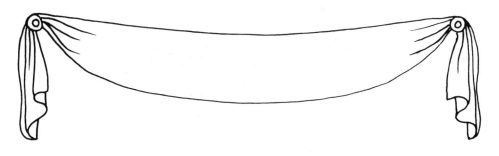

Skits with Unusual Effects

Some skits depend for their entertainment value on unusual effects, such as weird objects pulled from a patient's stomach during an operation, or a six-person "caterpillar" cavorting across the stage. These may require a bit more work in collecting props than the other skits in this book.

52.

The Very Hungry Caterpillar

CAST: Caterpillar trainer, segments of the caterpillar.

PROPS: To make the caterpillar, fasten blankets or sheets together and stretch them over the backs of several kids who are bent over in line. Each kid should have a can of rocks or some other noisemaker. These "segments" of the caterpillar will need to keep a hand free to pass things back as the caterpillar eats.

ACTION: A trainer feeding a very long caterpillar makes a speech about how wonderful this catepillar is. It will eat anything. The trainer feeds it a box of cereal (actually an empty box). The cereal is put in the caterpillar's "mouth," stuffed under the blanket in front. The caterpillar players pass the box back under the blankets. As each person takes the box he should shake his noisemaker, arch his back, and bump around as if digesting the cereal. It looks to the audience as if the food is passing through the caterpillar's body. When the box reaches the end, the last player tosses the "empty" box out from under the covers at the caterpillar's rear. You can repeat this with a can of beans (toss out an empty can) or whatever you want to feed your caterpillar.

ENDING: The caterpillar is still hungry after all the food is gone, so it eats the trainer. Repeat the same bumping and noisemaking motion down the line. When the trainer reaches the end of the line he stays inside the caterpillar. His shirt, pants, shoes, and socks are tossed out of the caterpillar's rear. Have a duplicate set of clothes to toss out. The caterpillar belches loudly and walks off stage.

Variants

This skit has many variations. Sometimes the creature is a dragon, a "moon bug," or a slug rather than a caterpillar. Sometimes the creature is put through a series of tricks: standing on its right legs, left legs, chasing its tail, etc. Sometimes a dupe, or several dupes, are brought onstage and told to lie down. You can see the results of that variation in *The Pet Slug*, which follows.

The Pet Slug

CAST: The slug, the slug's trainers.

ACTION: Several slug trainers bring on their trained slug and deposit it in stage center. The slug is a player encased in a sleeping bag. On command the slug rolls over, leaps in the air slightly, and performs other tricks.

ENDING: A volunteer is brought from the audience and is told that the slug has been trained to crawl over a human body. The volunteer (dupe) lies down and the slug crawls across, leaving a dribble of water or a trail of brown cotton balls. The trainers are embarrassed and apologize. "Oh, we forgot to tell you. Our slug isn't potty trained yet!"

54.

The Enlarging Wall

CAST: Owner of the "Enlarging Wall," customers, accomplice.

SCENE: A wall large enough to hide an accomplice. A sheet strung up, or a large box can be used.

ACTION: The owner of the famous "Enlarging Wall" boasts that this wall is magic. For a small sum of money, belongings can be enlarged. Anything thrown over the wall will be returned in a larger size. Customers bring on items which they hope to have enlarged. Someone brings out a piece of string. This is tossed over the wall and a piece of rope flies back. A little teddy bear is tossed over and a big one comes back. Invent as many "enlargements" as you can think of. Perhaps a wash cloth becomes a towel, a small origami folded crane becomes a large one, etc.

ENDING: A customer throws a glass of water over the wall (or spits over the wall). The wall owner shouts, "Oh, NO!" and runs for it. The customer stands there dumbly and is hit with a bucket of water that sloshes back over the wall.

Variant

Enlarging machine.

55.

The Spit Skit

CAST: Announcer, a group of world champion spitters, an assistant at the back of the audience.

SCENE: World spitting championship.

ACTION: The announcer introduces each famous spitter. Here's an example: "This is Nathan Dodge from Mercer Island, Washington. We are thrilled to have Nathan here with us today. He is going to perform his world championship loop-the-loop spit. Are you nervous, Nathan?" Do a big sports build-up. Nathan steps to the front of the stage and pretends to execute a gigantic spit. Both announcer and Nathan follow the imaginary spit with their eyes, head, and body as it soars into the air and loops the loop. The announcer praises Nathan and introduces the next contestant. You can invent as many spits as you like. Try the longest spit in the world, the highest spit, the shortest spit, the slowest, etc.

ENDING: Introduce the champion spitter who can spit "around the world!" The spitter prepares, turns his back to the audience, and spits. The spitters all exclaim as the spittle passes Hawaii . . . Japan . . . Russia . . . Europe . . . New York . . . Chicago . . . and returns to wherever you are. Just then your assistant tosses a spray of water into the audience from the back. Announcer calls, "Whooops! That one didn't quite make it all the way back to the stage. Sorry, folks!"

56.

The Fancy Pitchers

CAST: An announcer, several fancy pitchers.

SCENE: A ball field.

ACTION: The announcer introduces a fancy pitcher. Use lots of hype, sports-announcer style. "This is Nate Potter, the world famous baseball pitcher. Nate is going to show us his incredible curve ball pitch." Nate winds up and pitches. Announcer and Nate follow the imaginary pitch with their eyes. If you are in a dark enough space you can trace the path of the pretended pitch with a flashlight beam. Various pitchers come on and throw fancy pitches: fast ball, split-fingered slider, knuckleball, etc.

ENDING: The last pitcher throws an around-the-world ball. All follow it offstage left with their eyes, calling, "WOW. There it goes. It's passing Hawaii . . . flying over China . . . flying over Africa . . . etc. . . . crossing the Rocky Mountains. . . . ." Suddenly a baseball flies onstage from offstage right and hits the pitcher in the back. ". . . and it's BACK from around the world!"

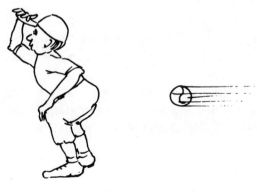

The Operation

CAST: Doctor, intern, nurses, patient.

SCENE: An operating room. A patient is on a table, hidden under a sheet.

ACTION: The intern announces that the famous surgeon, Dr. So-and-So, is about to operate. The doctor comes on stage with much fanfare and begins to operate. She pulls out a series of absurd items from the patient's stomach: a wrench . . . a toilet plunger . . . yards of rope . . . etc. Each time the doctor exclaims, "Oh, I see the trouble *now*," but there is always more to pull out.

ENDING: The doctor pulls out something very tiny and exclaims, "Oh, it was just the *appendix* causing all this trouble." The doctor dumps everything else back in and sews the patient up.

Variants

Sometimes the skit ends with the intern pulling out a tin can and holding it up. "Why, here's the trouble. It appears to be a can, sir." (Cancer).

This skit can be performed in silhouette behind a sheet, with a light source casting shadows. In that case, the objects pulled from the stomach can be cardboard cutouts, held up before the light.

You might want to add disgusting sound effects as the doctor operates. Try the ripping sound of a knife plunged into a cabbage, the scraping of metal on a bone, etc.

58.

Her Son's Operation

CAST: A mother, doctor, nurses, patient.

SCENE: An operating room. A patient on a table, hidden under a sheet.

ACTION: A mother is watching a doctor operate on her son. She tells the audience that this is her son, and that she is worried. The doctor removes a series of gross things from the sheet-covered patient. The mother exclaims in horror at each sight and almost faints. The nurses carry the disgusting material off the stage in trays, help support the fainting mother, etc. The doctor can remove long strands of spaghetti, a whole canned tomato dripping "blood," an actual soup bone with meat hanging in shreds, etc. Any disgusting stuff you can get your hands on will do.

ENDING: The doctor sews the patient up and the mother begs, "Doctor, Doctor, will my Johnny get well?" The doctor looks puzzled, consults the hospital bracelet on the patient's wrist. "Johnny? Johnny? This patient is Danny. My next patient is Johnny. Want to stay and watch me operate?" The mother faints dead away.

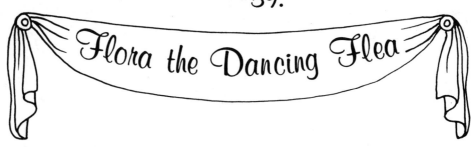

CAST: Flea trainer, onlookers, an imaginary flea.

SCENE: A flea circus. Some equipment for Flora's performance.

ACTION: A flea trainer is demonstrating the tricks of marvelous Flora the Dancing Flea to a small audience. As the trainer tells of Flora's leaps, both trainer and onlookers follow her movements with their eyes and exaggerated head movements. "Now, ladies and gentlemen, Flora will jump from this platform to that platform. Are you ready, Flora? Get ready. Get set. *Jump!*" All follow the trajectory of the imaginary Flora's jump. You can expand this skit as much as you want. It requires practice to coordinate all movements of your onlookers and the trainer. You might use several trainers, letting them take turns putting Flora through new tricks.

ENDING: Flora escapes and jumps onto the head of an audience member, possibly a dupe in the real audience. The trainer rushes to recover her. Searching through the hair where Flora has come to roost, he comes up with a flea, examines it, and mutters, "Why, *that's* not Flora!" You can expand this by finding numerous fleas which are not Flora. Finally, "There you are, Flora. Let's take your new friends home and start training."

Variant

Flora's tricks are demonstrated to an onlooker who exclaims, "Wonderful!" and claps . . . "Ooops! Sorry, Flora."

60.

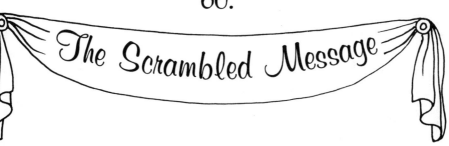

The Scrambled Message

CAST: Enough letter carriers to spell out your message. Some may hold more than one letter if necessary.

ACTION: All come on stage. Each carries a sign with one large letter of the alphabet. They mill around, then try to form words. They form the wrong words at first, shake their heads, and try again. You can play music to enliven this. Certain letters might have their own personalities and refuse to stay in place, etc.

ENDING: Eventually the letters organize themselves into the right sequence and spell out a message for the audience—"CAMP HUSTON IS THE GREATEST!" or maybe, "NO MORE MACARONI AND CHEESE!"

Variant

You can use a "director" to help arrange the letter carriers. This should be a clownlike figure who keeps getting everything wrong. Or you could ask someone from the audience to solve the puzzle and figure out what the letters spell. You might encourage the audience to shout out suggestions to the person trying to arrange the letters.

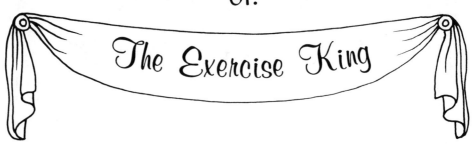

The Exercise King

CAST: The exercise king, his trainees, announcer.

ACTION: The announcer introduces the world famous expert on exercise —The Exercise King—who will lead the group in muscle-building exercises. Sometimes this is called the "Jane Fonda Workout" or you can substitute the name of a lazy counselor. The Exercise King, followed by his trainees, leads the audience in a series of silly exercises, such as exercising the elbow, the jaw, the ears, the nose, the big toe, etc.

ENDING: The Exercise King now asks everyone to combine the exercises and try to do them all at once. As the audience wiggles around foolishly, The Exercise King solemnly congratulates them on how much more fit they look now, and exits.

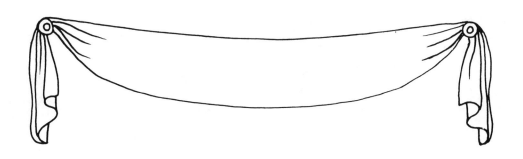

Mixed-Up Body Skits

This skit form can be adapted in many ways. The idea is for two people to perform as one individual. The hands of one feed the face of the second, etc. This can be done with only one (two-person) character, or you can set up several teams on the stage to perform at the same time. Sometimes the person whose head shows in the skit acts as narrator, or you might want to use a third person to announce the skit and narrate the action. Several possibilities for this mixed-up body skit are given here. You can probably think of more.

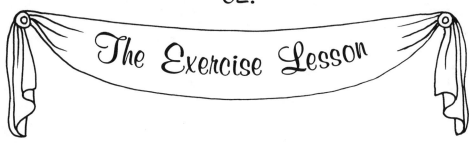

The Exercise Lesson

CAST: Two persons, or several teams of two each.

SCENE: A gym.

SET UP: One person lies flat on his back on the floor; the other kneels astride him facing his feet. A blanket covers the knees of the kneeling person. Another blanket covers the head and body of the reclining person, except for his legs. It appears that the legs belong to the kneeling individual.

ACTION: The kneeling person gives instruction for the exercises: "Now I will demonstrate the toe-touching routine." As he demonstrates, the leg person doesn't cooperate, jerking his toes out of the way, and causing problems for the narrator. The narrator, on the other hand, may announce actions which give the "legs" trouble: "I will now demonstrate holding both legs off the ground for five minutes." Perform several mixed-up exercises in this way.

ENDING: You can close by saying simply, "This concludes my exercise lesson. Thank you very much," and bowing from the "waist." Or you can ask the "legs" to do something so impossible that they rebel, yank themselves out from under you, and walk off.

63.

The Beauty Lesson

CAST: Two persons, or several couples.

SCENE: A beauty school.

SET UP: One person sits or stands behind another. The person in front wears a large shirt backwards, fastened around the neck. The person behind reaches around the front person into the arms of the shirt, becoming the "hands." The person behind can be covered by a drape, or two assistants can hold up a sheet as a backdrop behind the head of the speaking performer, draped so the head of the "hands" performer cannot be seen. This can also be performed with a huge sheet draped around both performers, like a beautician's cape.

ACTION: The person in front announces a beauty lesson and begins to give instructions for applying makeup. The "hands" apply the makeup. Since the person applying the makeup cannot see the face, this can become very funny. Apply lipstick, base, powder, eyebrow pencil, rouge, comb the hair, etc. Avoid eye makeup, as it could be dangerous.

ENDING: After creating a mess, announce that this concludes your beauty demonstration. Invite any audience members who would like a similar makeup job to see you after the performance.

64.

The Cooking Lesson

CAST: Two persons, or several couples.

SCENE: A cooking school.

SET UP: Same as for "The Beauty Lesson."

ACTION: The person whose head is visible to the audience narrates the cooking demonstration. If you are using several teams, let each team demonstrate one step of the process. You can be baking a cake, making fudge, whatever you like. It needs to be a dish that you can feed to your "speaking half" as a sample. As the narrator describes the process, the "hands" perform the pouring and mixing. Include an egg to crack. The "hands" might attempt to crack it on the chin of the narrator. Add flour, measure out sugar and salt, pour in water. Accidently spill a little of everything on the narrator.

ENDING: The "hands" give the talking "head" a taste of the concoction. The "head" resists tasting but finally is forced to take a bite. The "head" pretends to love it, tells the audience how wonderful it tastes, and invites them to come up for a sample after the show.

65.

The Big Date

CAST: Two persons to make up girl's body, two persons to make up boy's body, a narrator. You may add more couples if you like.

SCENE: The homes of a boy and a girl.

SET UP: Arrange actors as in "The Beauty Lesson."

ACTION: A boy is on one side of the stage getting ready for his date. A girl is getting ready on the other side of the stage. A narrator tells the audience about the proper preparation for a date as the characters act it out: "It is important to brush your teeth before going out." The "hands" reaching around from behind brush the "head's" teeth. They can wash faces, brush hair, part hair, put on perfume or aftershave. The girl can put on makeup, the boy can shave. Be sure they end up with hair messed up and makeup crooked.

ENDING: The narrator says, "And now . . . ready for the big date! They meet!" Each turns and looks at the other and shrieks.

The Dinner Date

CAST: A boy (made of two people), a girl (made of two people), a waiter. Use more than one couple if you like.

SCENE: A restaurant.

SET UP: Same as for "The Beauty Lesson."

ACTION: A boy and a girl are having dinner at a restaurant. The waiter keeps bringing them new dishes to eat. They try to carry on polite conversation, while their "hands" stuff food into their mouths. Provide plenty of napkins. Each can tell the other, such things as "You have a little spinach on your chin," in hopes of getting the "hands" to clean them up a little.

ENDING: Waiter comes on with a shaving cream pie, obviously designed to be slapped in someone's face. The "heads" say quickly, "We decided to SKIP DESSERT. That will be all, waiter! THIS ENDS OUR SKIT."

    If you decide to have the waiter serve gross things and snicker about them all along, you might have the dining couple complain about the pie, call the waiter over, and push it in *his* face.

Bizarre Body Parts

These skits use faces created from unusual parts of the body. The action can be a simple silly song or poem, or the "actor" can tell a joke or two. The humor comes from the unusual performer. Keep the action short. Here are some sample "bizarre body parts."

67.

Dancing Knee Dolls

Paint faces on the knees of the performers. Use dresses to dress the legs as dolls, with the arms of the dresses stuffed to bulge out. You could also dress the dolls in crepe paper, cloth, or other real clothing. Cover the upper legs and body with a sheet. Direct a flashlight (spotlight) onto each knee doll as it dances.

68.

Stomach Faces

Cover the heads and torsos of the performers with pillow cases decorated to look like hair or fancy hats. Paint faces on the performers' stomachs. Rig up clothing with the necks at the performers' waists. The actors can mime a song or perform a silly comedy routine. A fashion show performed in this manner is also effective.

69.

Chin Faces

Performers arrange themselves upside down with a drape covering the body except for mouth and chin. This can be done by lying flat on a tabletop with the head hanging over toward the audience. Keep the skit short, as you can't hold this position for long. Place sunglasses just below the chin in front of the neck for "eyes." The chin becomes the nose, the mouth is the mouth—but upside down so you must frown to smile, smile to frown. You can cover the eyes, or just keep them closed and they will not be noticed. The "chin face" makes a short silly speech or sings a humorous song. Several "chin faces" in a row can form a singing group, or mime a recording.

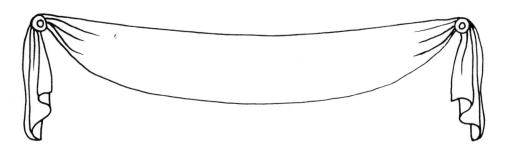

Skits as Melodramas

The melodrama, an early form of American theater, never fails to entertain. The audience is encouraged to hiss or boo the villain and cheer the hero. With this type of audience participation it is possible to create a successful skit from any story which has a heroine, a hero, and a villain. Two samples are included here. You could use the melodrama form to make up a skit of your own.

The Lighthouse Keeper's Daughter

CAST: Lighthouse keeper, his daughter, the villain, the hero, the lighthouse, the narrator, someone to lead the audience in cheering.

SCENE: A lighthouse in the sea.

ACTION: The narrator tells the story while it is acted out. Much of the action will have the actors going "round and round" the lighthouse, and the lighthouse itself must revolve, too. Be sure the actors have their directions clearly in mind before you start. They may end up dizzy, but that is part of the fun of the skit.

Meanwhile, a cheerleader coaches the audience to respond during the action. The audience should *hiss* whenever the villain, Evil Steve, is mentioned; sigh *"Ahhh"* for the Lighthouse Keeper's Daughter; cheer *"AT LAST!"* for Dudley Daring, Our Hero; and utter a fearful *"Oh, dear!"* for the Lighthouse Keeper. The cheerleader should rehearse the audience in these calls before the skit begins.

The lighthouse (a very tall person with a flashlight on his head), stands in the middle of the stage. The narrator describes the wild scene:

"Here we have a lonely lighthouse, beset by stormy seas. All alone the lighthouse stands, flashing its light round and round."

The lighthouse turns round and round until it gets dizzy and then stops.

"And in this lonely lighthouse lives the lonely Lighthouse Keeper (*Oh, dear!*) who climbs round and round the stairs. Round and round the stairs. Round and round the stairs.

Round and round the stairs, to reach the top of his lonely lighthouse. Which flashes its light round and round . . . round and round . . . round and round."

The lighthouse turns until it gets dizzy and then stops. Meanwhile the Lighthouse Keeper is still climbing round and round the lighthouse.

"The Lighthouse Keeper (*Oh, dear!*) takes his life savings from their hiding place atop the lonely lighthouse which turns . . ."

The lighthouse motions frantically for the narrator *not* to say the part which comes next. He stops just in time to save the dizzy lighthouse from revolving again.

"But HARK! Who is coming? It is the villain, Evil Steve!" (*hiss*).

Evil Steve comes onstage with back to the lighthouse, rowing a boat. He chortles evilly and rows madly for the lighthouse. Arriving, he ties his boat, gets out, and begins to climb around and around the lighthouse tower.

"Evil Steve (*hiss*) climbs round and round and round and round and round and round and round and round . . . to the very top of the lonely lighthouse whose light flashes round and round and round and round and . . . . *Meanwhile* . . . the Lighthouse Keeper (*Oh, dear!*) has picked up his *life savings* and started to climb down the stairs of the lonely lighthouse . . . round and round and round and round and . . . *suddenly* . . . Evil Steve (*hiss*) BUMPS into the Lighthouse Keeper (*Oh, dear!*) . . . GRABS the money from the Lighthouse Keeper (*Oh, dear!*) . . . and back down the stairs runs Evil Steve (*hiss*). While the lonely lighthouse flashes its light round and round and round and round and . . . Evil Steve (*hiss*) runs round and round and round and round . . . the poor Lighthouse Keeper (*Oh, dear!*) sits with his head going . . . round and round and round and round . . . . BUT WHAT IS THIS? The Lighthouse Keeper's Daughter (*Aaaaahh!*) comes."

From offstage comes the Lighthouse Keeper's Daughter, rowing daintily. All freeze as she approaches. She ties up her boat, gets out, and begins to climb the stairs. Suddenly all go into motion again. The narrator, who has been transfixed by the sight of the Lighthouse Keeper's Daughter, picks up the story once again.

"The Lighthouse Keeper's Daughter (*Aaaaahh!*) climbs the lonely lighthouse . . . round and round and round and . . . . while Evil Steve (*hiss*) climbs down the lighthouse . . . round and round and round and round and . . . And the Lighthouse Keeper (*Oh, dear!*), his head goes round and round and . . . oh, yes, I almost forgot, the lonely lighthouse flashes its light round and round and round and . . . . OH, NO! Evil Steve (*hiss*) meets the Lighthouse Keeper's Daughter (*Aaaaahh!*). Evil Steve (*hiss*) GRABS the Lighthouse Keeper's Daughter (*Aaaaahh!*). Evil Steve (*hiss*) carries off the Lighthouse Keeper's Daughter (*Aaaaahh!*). Down the lighthouse they go. Round and round and round and round and . . . while the Lighthouse Keeper's (*Oh, dear!*) head goes round and round and round and . . . the lonely lighthouse flashes its light . . . round and round and round and round and . . . . BUT HARK! WHO COMES? It is Dudley Daring . . . OUR HERO! (*AT LAST!*)"

All stand frozen as the narrator relates the coming of Dudley Daring.

"He rows toward the lonely lighthouse . . . Dudley Daring our hero (*AT LAST!*). He reaches the lonely lighthouse . . . Dudley Daring our hero (*AT LAST!*). He climbs the lonely lighthouse . . . Dudley Daring our hero (*AT LAST!*) . . . round and round and round and round . . . ."

All spring into motion again.

"While down the lighthouse comes Evil Steve (*hiss*) dragging the Lighthouse Keeper's Daughter (*Aaaaahh!*) . . . round and round and round and round . . . as the Lighthouse Keeper's head (*Oh, dear!*) goes round and round and . . . .

and the lonely lighthouse flashes its light round and round and round and . . . . HALT! Dudley Daring our hero! (*AT LAST!*) MEETS Evil Steve (*hiss*). Dudley Daring our hero! (*AT LAST!*) BASHES Evil Steve (*hiss*). Dudley Daring our hero! (*AT LAST!*) VANQUISHES Evil Steve (*hiss*).

Evil Steve is brought to kneel at the feet of Dudley Daring.

"The Lighthouse Keeper's Daughter (*Aaaaahh!*) runs up the stairs . . . round and round and round and . . . to her father, the Lighthouse Keeper (*Oh, dear!*), whose head stops going round and round . . . as Dudley Daring our hero! (*AT LAST!*) runs up the stairs . . . round and round and round . . . dragging Evil Steve (*hiss*) . . . round and round and round . . . until they STOP! And Evil Steve (*hiss*) gives BACK the stolen life savings of the Lighthouse Keeper (*Oh, dear!*) . . . and the Lighthouse Keeper's Daughter (*Aaaaahh!*) gives her poor father a kiss . . . and . . . why not . . . a kiss to Dudley Daring our hero! (*AT LAST!!!!*). While the lonely lighthouse flashes its light round . . . and round and round and . . . . "

71.

Who'll Pay the Rent?

CAST: Villainous landlord, poor maiden, maiden's poor family, hero.

SCENE: Lowly home on which rent has not been paid. Each cast member has a single prop, a paper bow. Accordion-pleat a piece of paper and hold it in the middle for your bow.

ACTION: A poor maiden and her poor family are eating a poor meal in their poor home. The maiden holds her bow beside her head coyly as she speaks. Her baby sister holds her bow on top of her head as she speaks. Grandma holds her bow as if gathering hair behind her neck. The hero hold his bow as a bow tie. The villain holds his bow under his nose as a mustache as he speaks. Add more characters if you like.

Villain knocks on door and maiden opens it.

Villain: "Your rent is DUE."

Maiden: "But I can't pay the rent."

Villain: "But you MUST pay the rent."

Maiden: "But I CAN'T pay the rent."

Villain: "But you MUST pay the rent."

Grandma: "But she CAN'T pay the rent."

Villain: "But she MUST pay the rent."

Baby: "But she CAN'T pay the rent."

Villain: "But she MUST pay the rent."

This should be delivered rapidly with great exaggeration, and much repetition.

ENDING: All finally insist together, "BUT SHE CAN'T PAY THE RENT!"

> *Villain:* "But she MUST pay the rent!"
>
> Hero enters. "I'LL pay the rent!"
>
> *Maiden:* "My HERO!"
>
> *All:* "Our HERO!"
>
> Villain to audience: "CURSES. Foiled again!"

> Villain slinks offstage as hero and maiden embrace and all cheer again, "OUR HERO!"

"Ah!"

CAST: Hero, heroine, thief, police, maid, father, mother. You can add grandparents, cook, more maids, more police.

SCENE: A living room.

ACTION: No word is spoken throughout except "Ah." Maid is dusting living room singing in "Ah's." She sees the hero coming and gives a disgusted "Ah" and leaves. Hero and heroine meet with ecstatic "Ahs." They sit down to smooch with many "Ahs." He gives her a ring: "Ahhh." He must leave. Parents enter after he goes and the girl shows them the ring. Mother is delighted: "Aaahh!" Father is disgusted: "Aaaahhh." Girl puts the ring in a jewelry box and goes to bed. A thief enters: "Ah!" and takes the ring. The maid enters: "Ah! AAAAHHHHH!" and screams for help. Parents enter and scream. Thief panics: "Ah . . . Ahh . . . Ah" . . . and cannot escape.

ENDING: Hero rushes in with police: "Ah!" They capture thief. Thief leaves with cop. Family all sigh: "Aaaah." Hero and heroine fall into each others' arms: "Aaaahhh."

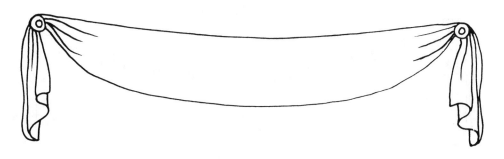

Skits From Commercials

Many humorous skits have been created by poking fun at a popular commercial which everyone has seen on TV or in ads. Four of these "commercial skits" are included here. Once you get the idea you can probably think up skits of your own. It is important to base them on commercials which are generally popular, so that everyone can recognize them. For example skit number 73; "The Sesame Street Bus" will be effective as long as MacDonald's "two all-beef patties, special sauce, lettuce, cheese, pickles, onions, on a Sesame Seed bun is a recognizable commercial slogan. The best commercials to make fun of are those which have been overused until everyone is sick of them.

73.

The Sesame Street Bus

CAST: Bus driver, two Pattys, Ross, Lester Sleaze, policeman. Add other passengers if needed.

SCENE: A moving bus. Arrange chairs for driver and passengers. Place a sign saying "Sesame Street" on the front of the bus.

ACTION: The bus is moving when the driver stops and opens the door. Two very fat girls get on. Stuff their clothes with pillows. The first girl says to the driver, "Hi. I'm Patty." The second says, "Hi. I'm Patty, too." The driver replies: "Two Pattys, is it? A little obese, aren't you, Pattys? Well, take a seat." The driver drives on and stops again. A cool dude gets on. "Hi. I'm Ross. I'm SPECIAL, man." Driver: "Hi, Special Ross. Take a seat." Ross bops around and finally sits down. The bus stops again and Lester gets on. Lester tries to slip by without paying his fare but the driver catches him. "Lester, don't be a sleaze again. Pay your fare." Lester pays. The driver turns to the audience, "That's Lester Sleaze, in case you didn't know." Lester sits down, takes off his shoe and sock and begins picking at his bunions. The driver tells him, "That's disgusting, Lester, stop picking your bunions."

All the passengers begin to make a ruckus, talking at once and rioting around the bus. The driver tries to quiet them but begins to weave in traffic.

ENDING: A traffic cop stops the bus: "What's the meaning of this crazy driving?" The driver begs off: "I'm sorry, officer, but what would you do if you were stuck with . . . . two obese Pattys, Special Ross, Lester Sleaze, picking bunions on a SESAME STREET BUS!"

Dr. Bluebonnet

CAST: Dr. Bluebonnet, receptionist, nurse, patients.

SCENE: A doctor's office.

ACTION: A receptionist is sitting behind a desk in Dr. Bluebonnet's office. A patient comes in with a broken leg. "Is Dr. Bluebonnet in?" "No, he hasn't come in yet. Please lie down right over there and wait." The nurse helps arrange the patient on the floor. You can use blankets and pillows for the patients to lie on. One by one, more patients enter and ask for Dr. Bluebonnet. Each is told to lie down. The nurse arranges them in a group, lying side by side.

ENDING: Dr. Bluebonnet enters and asks if there are any patients to see him today. He is delighted to see the patients and assures them they will soon be better. Dr. Bluebonnet lies down at one end of the row of patients and begins to roll himself over the top of them. As he rolls past, both he and the patients sing out, "Everything's better . . . with Bluebonnet on it!" The patients jump up cured, bow, and go off.

NOTE: This skit is already dated as younger kids may not have heard the margarine jingle, "Everything's better with Blue Bonnet on it."

Takes a Lickin' and Keeps On Tickin'

CAST: Wristwatch demonstration team, strongmen, dog.

SCENE: Watch demonstration.

ACTION: A person wearing a sturdy wristwatch enters, removes the wristwatch, and holds it up for all to see. The wristwatch is laid on a log or cement block. A strongman enters carrying a sledgehammer or club. He bashes the watch, then leaves. The watch can be made of cardboard, or the club can be made of foam. The demonstrator holds up the unharmed watch and proudly shows it to the audience: "Takes a lickin' and keeps on tickin'!" Repeat this action with other watch wearers. The watch demonstrators can stand at the rear of the stage watching each new watch withstand the strongman's club.

ENDING: A smallish person comes on wearing a very dainty wristwatch. She places the watch on the log to be smashed. The onlookers gasp in horror as the strongman raises his club, but just in time the watch's owner springs up and stops the strongman. She runs off stage and returns leading her pet dog—an actor with ears and tail pinned on. The dog comes up, sniffs the watch, and begins to lick it. The watch is held up: "Takes a lickin' and keeps on tickin!" Everyone cheers.

Yellow Fingers

CAST: A king, knights, pages, a narrator, yellow fingers.

SCENE: A royal court.

ACTION: A narrator tells the story of a kingdom where a group of terrible "yellow fingers" have blocked the castle entrance and won't let anyone pass. The performers act this out as the narrator speaks. The gist of the story is that the king sends a knight to fight the yellow fingers. He fights valiantly, but the knight is slain. Another knight is sent and also is killed. Repeat these battles with several knights.

ENDING: At last no one is left but a lowly page of the court. The king sends him to a certain death, but as the page approaches the yellow fingers he is allowed to walk right through them. The narrator reports the moral of this story: "Let your pages do the walking through the yellow fingers."

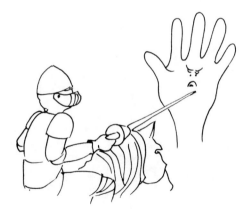

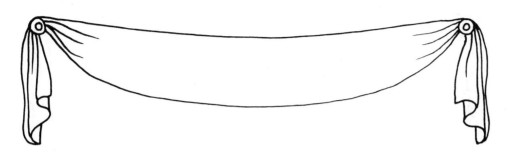

Skits from Jokes

Jokes can often be transformed into skits and skits are sometimes retold as jokes. Many of the skits in the "Trick Endings" section of this book also exist in joke form. Here are a few skits which were clearly created from jokes kids are telling today. By remembering some of the jokes you know, you may come up with other good ideas for skits.

To make a joke into a skit, decide who will play the various characters in the joke, go over the joke to make sure you know the action, then act it out, letting your characters improvise their own dialogue. Make sure that the punchline is clear. And be sure that the action includes all of the information the audience needs to appreciate the punchline. It helps to have a friend watch your skit before you give your big performance. Someone not taking part in the action can tell you if your skit is getting its humorous message across.

Abel's Fable

CAST: Ghost of Abel's Fable, several kids.

SCENE: Haunted room.

ACTION: A ghost is lurking in a haunted house. There is a pile of money on the table. The ghost wails and moans around the stage to establish a ghostly presence. A kid sneaks in and tries to take the money from the table. The ghost wails, "I am the Ghost of Abel's Fable. Put that money back on the table!" The kid flees in terror, leaving the money. Repeat this with others coming in to take the money.

ENDING: The last kid to enter is dressed in flashy clothes, and it is clear this kid takes no guff from anyone. The ghost wails as usual, "I am the Ghost of Abel's Fable. Put that money back on the table!" But this kid turns on the ghost and says, "Well, I am the Ghost of Davy Crockett. I'm putting this money right in my pocket." The kid takes the money, threatens the ghost, and the ghost flees.

Taking the Penguins for a Ride

CAST: "Penguin keeper," penguins, police officer.

SCENE: A highway.

ACTION: A man with a busload of penguins chugs across the stage. A police officer stops the driver and asks, "Where are you taking these penguins?" The driver replies, "I'm taking them to the beach." The officer advises him to take them to the zoo instead. The driver obliges, changes direction, and chugs off with the penguins.

ENDING: The driver chugs back on stage with his busload of penguins. The police officer stops him again: "I thought I told you to take these penguins to the zoo!" The driver replies, "I did. They had a great time. Now I'm taking them to the movies."

The Ghost of the Two White Eyes

CAST: Ghost, kids looking for a room to spend the night.

SCENE: A haunted house.

ACTION: A ghost haunts the stage. One by one, kids enter with their sleeping bags. Each time one spreads out a bag the ghost suddenly appears and begins to wail, "I am the Ghost of the Two White Eyes . . . . " Each kid is terrified and flees. Repeat this with as many kids as you wish.

ENDING: The last kid to enter the haunted house ignores the ghost and goes about the business of laying out the sleeping bag and preparing to spend the night. The ghost begins to wail, "I am the Ghost of the Two White Eyes . . . . " This kid just ignores him. The ghost keeps wailing, becoming more and more annoying. Finally the kid turns on the ghost: "You may be the Ghost of the Two White Eyes now—but if you don't shut up, you'll be the Ghost of the One BLACK Eye!" He threatens the ghost with his fist and the ghost flees.

NOTE: This is also told as a popular ghost story or joke at Halloween.

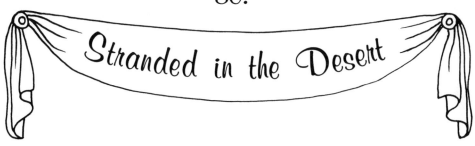

Stranded in the Desert

CAST: Three or more stranded people, a genie.

SCENE: A desert.

ACTION: A thirsty group trudges through the desert. They complain of their thirst and mourn that they will never reach water. Suddenly one finds a magic lamp in the sand. They rub the lamp and a genie appears. The genie grants each of them one wish. The first says, "I wish I were back home eating dinner!" He whirls offstage en route back home. They are all excited now and clamor for a turn: "Wow! It really works!" The second wishes to be home watching her favorite TV show. She whirls offstage too. Repeat this until all of the stranded people except one have been whisked away.

ENDING: The last stranded person is left alone in the desert. He looks around, sits down, and says how lonely he is now that his friends are gone. He wishes they were all back with him. The escaped friends whirl back in from offstage. All look at the last wisher, realize what he has done, and chase him offstage in a rage.

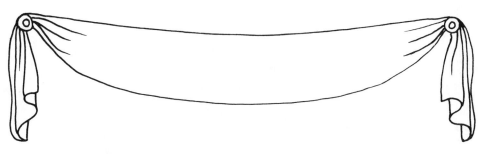

Skits from Stories

Like jokes, folktales and short stories can be used as skit material. To make a skit from a story, simply decide who will play each character, read the story through carefully noting all the important twists of the plot, and then begin acting it out. Let the characters improvise their lines. Add a few bits of creative costuming, rehearse a couple of times, and you are ready to perform. Remember, this is not a rehearsed play, this is just a short, humorous skit. Feel free to ad lib as you perform. Let each player develop his or her character for the greatest possible humorous effect. Sometimes when a punchline falls flat a skit can still be a big hit because of the entertaining way it was performed.

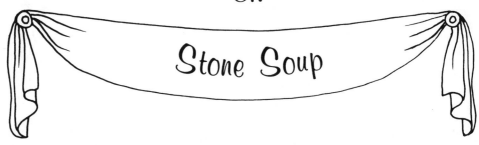

Stone Soup

CAST: Clever kid with stone, leader, as many other kids as you like.

SCENE: A cookout.

ACTION: Kids come in from a hike and begin getting out their lunches. Each shows the fantastic food he or she has brought. The clever kid pulls out an unsavory lunch of stale bread and peanut butter, or such. She examines this lunch, tells the audience what a rotten lunch it is and tosses it away. Then she picks up a stone, asks the leader for a stewpot, builds a fire, fills the pot with water, and begins to boil the stone. The other kids crowd around curiously while the clever kid talks on and on about how marvelous this stone soup is going to taste. She says the others can share it if they contribute something to the pot. One puts in carrots, another potatoes, another a piece of ham, etc. When the soup is done, each gets a bowl full and they all say how wonderful it is and praise the soupmaker.

ENDING: The clever kid gets up, tosses her stone in the air and catches it, saying, "There's nothing to it. It's just a matter of finding the right stone—and the right kids!" Winks at the audience and exits.

The Wide-Mouthed Frog

CAST: A Wide-Mouthed Frog, a Giant Bullfrog, and other creatures.

SCENE: A swamp.

ACTION: The Wide-Mouthed Frog hops on stage grinning broadly. The frog must keep its mouth in this wide grin until the end of the skit. The frog meets a wasp and introduces himself: "Hello, who are you?" Wasp: "I'm a little wasp." Frog: "Well, I'm a WIDE-MOUTHED FROG! I eat little wasps." Wasp: "Then good-bye, Wide-Mouthed Frog." The wasp leaves hurriedly. One by one other creatures come onstage and carry on the same conversation. You can use dragonflies, grasshoppers, any insect or small creature that is easy to mime.

ENDING: A giant bullfrog hops intimidatingly on stage. The Wide-Mouthed Frog spies him and says, "Hello. Who are you?"

"I'm the Giant Bullfrog. Who are YOU?"

"I'm the WIDE-MOUTHED FROG. I . . . "

The bullfrog interrupts. "Wonderful! I EAT wide-mouthed frogs for LUNCH!"

The Wide-Mouthed Frog suddenly purses lips into a very tiny circle and says, "Ooo . . ! " He turns and hops off stage muttering to audience with tiny pursed lips, "He eats wide-mouthed frogs for lunch . . . . Ooo . . !"

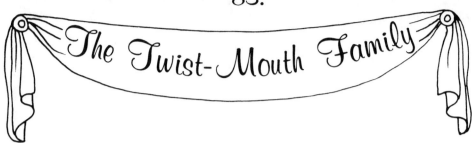

The Twist-Mouth Family

CAST: Policeman, many members of the Twist-Mouth family. The members of the Twist-Mouth family must twist their mouths into peculiar positions so that when they blow at a candle, the air will be directed away from the flame.

SCENE: The bedroom of the Twist-Mouth family after dark. They hold a single candle. They should be dressed in nightshirts, pajamas, etc.

ACTION: Papa Twist-Mouth calls his family around him and says goodnight to each with a kiss. He is holding the candle. "Say goodnight, Mama Twist-Mouth." Mama Twist-Mouth says, "Goodnight, Papa Twist-Mouth," and gives him a kiss. Papa says, "Say goodnight, Baby Twist-Mouth." Baby says, "Goodnight, Papa Twist-Mouth." Etc. When all have said goodnight Papa says, "Now it's time to blow out the candle and go to bed." He blows and blows but as his lower lip sticks out, the air goes up and away from the candle. Mama Twist-Mouth says she will try. Her upper lip sticks out and the air goes down away from the candle. Sister tries, but blows to the side, etc. They begin to wail, "We can't go to bed. We can't blow out our candle."

     A policeman passing by hears them and calls up to ask what is going on. They tell him and he comes up to help. He blows out the candle. (If it is possible to darken the stage at this point, do so). Everyone thanks the kind policeman. Mama Twist-Mouth says, "Papa Twist-Mouth, show the kind policeman out. Oh, you'd better light a candle so you don't trip on the stairs." Papa lights the candle and shows the policeman out. He returns to the family. "At last. Now we can all go to bed."

ENDING: All point to the lighted candle in despair. But baby toddles up
with a full chamber pot and offers it. Papa dips the candle into
the pot and extinguishes it with a sizzle. All sigh in unison. For
another ending, baby can snuff the candle out with thumb and
forefinger.

*NOTE: You will need to get permission to use a lighted candle for
this skit.*

The Bad Exchange

CAST: A musician who wants to practice in peace and quiet, a carpenter, a plumber, and a messenger. To expand the cast use more than one plumber, carpenter, and/or musician.

SCENE: A musician's studio. On one side is a carpenter's shop and on the other is a plumber's shop—or you could invent other noisy neighbors.

ACTION: The musician begins to practice, saying how much this quiet environment is needed for concentration. The carpenter comes in next door and goes to work, hammering and sawing loudly. The plumber comes in on the other side and goes to work, pounding loudly on the metal pipes. The musician is distraught and sends a messenger to tell the plumber that she will pay $100.00 for the plumber to move somewhere else. The same offer is sent to the carpenter. Both accept. Each takes the money, packs up her gear, and leaves to find somewhere else to live. Out on the street they meet and tell each other their troubles. Since each is looking for a new shop and each has a shop to rent, they decide to exchange shops. Meanwhile the musician practices on, blissfully.

ENDING: The carpenter moves into the plumber's former shop, and the plumber moves into the carpenter's former shop. They both begin to hammer and pound! The musician screams and runs from the stage, driven insane.

The Wise Man

CAST: A man who can't sleep, a Wise Man, farm animals, sound effects person.

ACTION: A man, unable to sleep, is tossing and turning in his bed. He complains of the noise. A sound effects person offstage makes quiet sounds of leaves swishing, wind blowing gently, perhaps a board creaking quietly. The man says he can't sleep with all this racket. Finally he gets up and goes to the Wise Man for help. The Wise Man sits behind a table with a big book to consult. He tells the sleepless man, "This is a serious problem. But I can help you. What you need is a CAT. Go. Get a cat."

The man buys a cat and takes it home. Someone can come onstage and sell it to him, or he can simply go offstage and come back with the cat. The cat, of course, is another actor with drawn-on whiskers and pinned-on ears. The man goes back to bed. The leaves, wind, and board continue to make sounds, and now the cat meows. The sleepless man goes back to the Wise Man, and is told to get a dog. He buys a dog and comes home. He tries to sleep. The leaves, wind, and board continue; the cat meows; and the dog barks. The sleepless man continues to visit the Wise Man and is told to get another animal each time. At last he has a cow, a horse, a pig, etc. Add whatever animals you like as long as they are noisy.

ENDING: Finally the sleepless man tells the Wise Man that he cannot stand this any longer. The Wise Man tells him to go home and get rid of the cat, dog, cow, horse, etc. He leads the animals offstage and comes back. He lies down. The wind blows gently, the board squeaks softly, the leaves swish. "Ahhhh," he sighs. "Silence at last." He falls asleep.

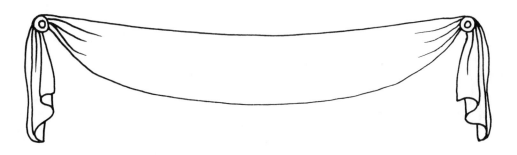

Skits from Songs

A few examples of skits made from songs are included here. It is easy to make up a skit using a silly song. Just practice the song a few times and add a bit of costuming. Song skits can be performed in different ways. Sometimes the entire group sings the song together. Sometimes a clowning song leader directs the group. Or you could assign parts to the characters in a song and act it out as you sing. Think over the funny songs you know and you'll probably come up with several which make good skits.

86.

The Mother Goose Singers

CAST: Many singers, a master of ceremonies, a clowning singer.

ACTION: The Mother Goose Singers come on and the master of ceremonies announces that they will take requests to sing nursery rhymes. Let the audience shout out suggestions and the M.C. can select one. As the chorus sings the rhyme, the clowning singer jumps out in the middle of the song and takes over the direction, changing the words to "They threw it out the window." Here is an example. Use any tune you like.

> "Old Mother Hubbard went to her cupboard
> To get her poor dog a bone.
> When she got there, the cupboard was bare
> And so the poor dog had none.
> She threw it
> She threw it
> She threw it out the window.
> When she got there, the cupboard was bare.
>   (repeat third line of rhyme here)
> So she threw it out the window."

Try other nursery rhymes using this form and see what silly effects you can get. Just remember to use the third line of the rhyme in the "threw it out the window" chorus. You get choruses such as, "He stuck in his thumb and pulled out a plumb . . . And threw it out the window!" and "Along came a spider and sat down beside her . . . She threw it out the window!"

    Practice beforehand using Mother Goose rhymes you think the audience might ask for. You might end with a parody of your school or camp song set to this tune.

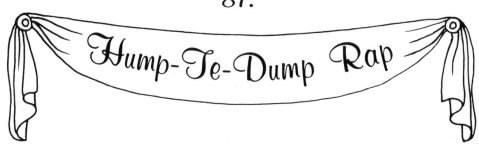

87.

Hump-Te-Dump Rap

CAST: Rappers.

ACTION: This is a rap. All can perform it together, or each performer can take one verse with all joining on the chorus. The audience could join on the chorus too. Use any nursery rhyme for this. Simply substitute the formula below for the last line. chant this as a rap, as you can see in these examples.

Rap: "Little Miss Muffet sat on a tuffet
          Eating her curds and whey.
          Along came a spider and sat down beside her
          And said, 'Hey, ain't that funky now!'"

Chorus: "HUMP-te-DUMP
          HUMP-te-DUMP-te-DUMP-te
          HUMP-te-DUMP
          HUMP-te-DUMP-te-DUMP-te."

Rap: "Little Bo Peep has lost her sheep
          And doesn't know where to find them.
          Leave them alone and they will come home
          Saying, 'Hey, ain't that funky now!'"

Chorus: HUMP-te-DUMP," etc.

Carry this on as long as you like, substituting other Mother Goose rhymes for the verse each time.

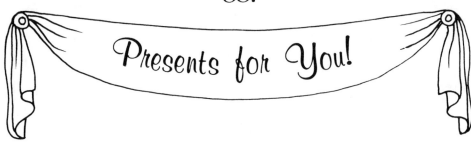

Presents for You!

CAST: As many singers as you like; an announcer.

SCENE: A row of singers. Each singer should have a handful of something to toss to the audience: candy, nuts, flowers, balloons, paper airplanes, confetti, etc.

ACTION: The announcer tells the audience that this group has brought gifts for them. The first singer sings:

> "My name is Jenny
> My name is Jenny
> My name is Jenny
> And I've brought candy for you!"

Use any tune you like. The tune for "Mary Had a Little Lamb" works. Each singer repeats this song, using his or her own name. Each throws something different into the audience.

ENDING: The last singer sings:

> "My name is Julie
> My name is Julie
> My name is Julie
> I've brought rotten eggs for you!"

and throws eggs at the audience! Prepare the eggs in advance by poking a small hole in one end and removing the runny insides. Do this early so they can dry before skit time. If you like you can refill them with paper confetti and reseal the hole, but the breaking egg shells alone will be quite effective, as the audience thinks they are real eggs!

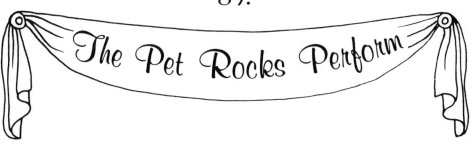

The Pet Rocks Perform

CAST: Any number of rock trainers.

SCENE: A table on which the rocks perform. It can be covered with a drape, so the trainers cannot be seen.

ACTION: The trainers enter and introduce their pet rocks with much ado. The rocks are placed on a table to perform in full view of the audience. The trainers duck out of sight behind the table. In thin "rock" voices the trainers sing for the rocks. They reach up a hand now and then to execute a quick leap or a bow with the rocks. Any silly song can be sung, but a good one to use is "I'm a Rock!" sung to the tune of "I'm a Nut!"

ENDING: The rocks bow. Then the trainers emerge and bow too.

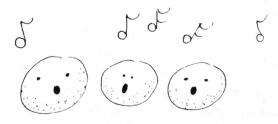

Variant

Use peanuts singing, "I'm a Nut!"

A-Boom-Chic-A-Boom!

CAST: Leader and cheering chorus dressed in unusual styles.

ACTION: Leader directs the chorus in a cheer:

"I said a-BOOM-chic-a-BOOM!
I said a-BOOM-chic-a-BOOM!
"I said a-BOOM-chic-a-MONGA-chic-a-MONGA-chic-a-BOOM."

After a few cheers, one of the chorus jumps forward and orders, "One more time. Teeny-bopper style." The cheer is repeated in this exaggerated style. One by one, chorus members come forward and demand that the cheer be repeated in "their" style. Each can be dressed in that style. Examples: Baby style; punk rocker style; football player style; aerobics style; etc.

ENDING: End with a style named after your group: "Camp Huston style," "Cub Scout style," etc. Lead the audience as they join in this last cheer.

Variant

This can be used as a crowd warm-up exercise instead of a skit.

I'm a Little Teapot

CAST: Group of teapots.

ACTION: Actors place left hand on hip and extend right arm in air like a spout. One by one they step forward and sing with appropriate actions:

"I'm a little teapot, short and stout.
Here is my handle.
Here is my spout.

When I get all steamed up, then I shout.
Tip . . . me over
And pour me OUT."

ENDING: The last little teapot comes forward. This pot, which has BOTH hand on hips all along, sings:

"I'm a little teapot, short and stout.
Here is my handle . . .
Here is my . . . . "

The teapot gets confused as it doesn't seem to have a spout. It begins again, but stops at the same place. After a few tries the teapot comes to an awful conclusion: "Shoot . . . I'm a SUGAR BOWL!" and runs off stage crying.

Variant

This can be used as an activity song for the entire audience.

Silly Singers

To make a humorous song even funnier, you might use an unusual set-up for your singers. Try the following.

92.

Mixed Singing

For this skit you need a curtain or a sheet held behind the singers. Four female singers come on stage and begin to sing. However, they are only miming the words. The real singers are four guys hidden behind the curtain. You must practice to make this work. If you can provide a piano accompaniment it will be easier for the two groups to keep together.

93.

The Upside Down Singers

The singers are onstage. An announcer explains that they are going to sing upside down! They duck out of sight behind the curtain (a sheet held by two accomplices will do). Placing their hands in their shoes, they wobble the shoes above the curtain top. It should look as if they are having trouble standing on their heads and are about to topple over as they sing. This requires practice and you will need a director to help you get the motions right. To end the skit let one of the curtain holders become distracted and accidentally drop the curtain revealing the "upside down" singers in action.

94.

Mixed Body Singing

Fasten a shirt backwards around a singer's neck, leaving the sleeves empty. Let a second actor stand behind the singer with her arms through the shirt sleeves. A sheet can be draped over the head and body of the person behind, or two accomplices can hold the sheet as a screen behind the head of the singer. As the singer performs, the hands of the second person gesture. You can do this with several pairs of singers if you like. For other "mixed body" skits which could be adapted to music, see the "Mixed Body" section of this book.

Musical Ensembles

There are many ways to create a skit using a band. Here are a few suggestions. You can probably think of even more ways to perform with a real musical group or a clowning fake band.

95.

The Living Xylophone

The instrument consists of several kneeling performers. The player strikes each on the head with a mallet as if playing a xylophone. Each player utters a single note when struck. They perform a simple song such as "Twinkle, Twinkle Little Star" when played in this way.

96.

Balloon Orchestra

The players in the orchestra each hold a balloon. They blow up their balloons in unison, then let the air out a squeak at a time to the rhythm of some easily recognized tune such as "Jingle Bells" or "The Blue Danube Waltz." To end the skit all fill their balloons with air and on signal by the director let them loose.

97.

The One-Man Band

A group of people walk on stage carrying instruments as if they are going to play. They arrange themselves, get out their instruments—and then all hand the instruments to one person. This is the one-man band! The rest form the chorus and sing while the one-man band plays. Or they can all just sit and watch while he plays as many of the instruments as possible.

98.

Sour Notes

CAST: Director, accompanist, orchestra or chorus.

ACTION: The director tunes up the orchestra or chorus and they begin to make music. One by one each player hits a very sour note. Each time the director stops the music and throws the player off the stage. Repeat until only the accompanist and director are left.

ENDING: When all have been thrown off stage the director turns to the accompanist and begins a solo. The director hits a sour note and the accompanist jumps up and throws the director off stage. The accompanist comes back on stage with a satisfied look, bows to the audience, and exits.

The Kitchen Band

CAST: Any number of players, a band director.

ACTION: Players come on carrying an assortment of kitchen items: pots and pans, egg beaters, wooden spoons, etc. With much ado the director tunes them up. They play on their instruments the rhythmical accompaniment to a silly made-up song which they also sing off-key. Or they can simply play a jazzy tune.

ENDING: Simply play, bow, and exit. Or, have someone dressed up as a cook or a mother storm in, take back the utensils, and stalk off.

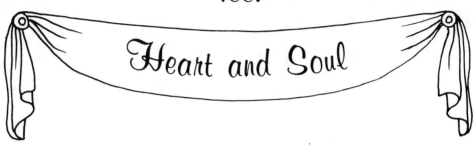

Heart and Soul

CAST: Piano player, lovers, jealous lover, sign carrier.

SCENE: A dance.

ACTION: The pianist plays "Heart and Soul" in varying keys, rhythms, and moods, as the actors perform. A sign carrier may pass across the stage to signal mood changes. The skit can include as many segments as you can think up. Try these:

SIGN	ACTION
THE LUNCH	Boy and girl enter, sit at table, dine pleasantly.
THE WALTZ	They get up and dance.
THE ARGUMENT	They have a disagreement.
THE JEALOUS LOVER	A third party enters and starts a row.
THE FIGHT	A fight erupts.
THE VICTORY	The true love wins and gloats.
THE END	The boy and girl are alone together at last.

101.

The Paper Bag Band

CAST: A group of players with instruments, cases, conductor.

SCENE: A recital hall.

ACTION: The players enter carrying their instrument cases. With much care they open their cases. Each removes a brown paper bag. Some are large, some small. The conductor raps the band to attention and all blow their bags open with a huge gust. Holding the bags in front of them, they begin to play by tapping on the sides of the open bags. The larger bags make a deeper sound. Use a variety of sizes for the most effective performance.

ENDING: All performers blow up their bags, hold the necks tight, and . . . POP them.

Collecting These Skits

I collected these skits mainly from students in the Seattle, Washington suburban communities of Bothell, Kirkland, Redmond, and Mercer Island during 1988. These kids had seen skits at school, especially during their fifth grade camping week, a required "Outdoor Education" event in Washington schools. Many had attended day camps as well, and all had been to overnight camps. The YMCA and scouting groups were especially important sources of skits.

By enlisting input from Girl Scouts, Boy Scouts, and veterans of church, music, and YMCA camps, I hoped to get a representative sampling of skit use in this area. After I had compiled a list of skits for possible inclusion in this book, I returned to several key informants and asked them to read the entire list, checking those skits they had seen. My informant sample was limited and my collecting technique was geared to produce a useful contemporary skit book. Still, in the absence of more scholarly approaches to skit-lore, this collection may be useful to the folklorist as well as to the producers and performers of skits.

To find out if these skits were popular in places other than the northwestern United States, I contacted the American Camping Association and asked counselors and camp directors around the country to write to me. Counselors with experience in California, Indiana, Iowa, Kentucky, Pennsylvania, Maryland, Massachusetts, Minnesota, New Hampshire, Ohio, Vermont, and Wisconsin replied. They are included in the "Skit Contributors" list, too. I was interested to see from their comments which skits are known throughout the country — but perhaps equally interesting was discovering which of those popular in the Seattle area had not been encountered elsewhere.

Skit Contributors

These are the kids and counselors who shared skits with me. I have given a number to each name. These numbers are used in the "Sources for Skits" section that follows. Ages of all the younger contributors are given following their names. My "key informants" have asterisks by their names. Counselors from outside the Seattle area who helped are listed under "American Camping Association Members."

KIDS

1. Cameron, Susie.* 16, Mercer Island, Wash.
2. Dodge, Nathan.* 14, and Tova Dodge, 17, Mercer Island, Wash.
3. Drew, Emily.* 14, Kirkland, Wash.
4. Ford, Rachel. 12, Bellevue, Wash.
5. Herlich, Wendy.* 14, Seattle, Wash.
6. Hill, Jennifer.* 12, Kirkland, Wash.
7. Jordan, Dominique.* 15, Kirkland, Wash.
8. Karnes, Heather.* 16, Mercer Island, Wash.
9. Kester, Lisa.* 16, Kirkland, Wash.
10. Lee, Tanya. 16, Bothell, Wash.
11. Lenox, April. 12, North Haven, Conn.
12. Long, Anthony.* 14, Bothell, Wash.
13. MacDonald, Jennifer.* 16, Kirkland, Wash.
14. MacDonald, Julie.* 14, Kirkland, Wash.
15. Mannon, Lee Anne. 16, Kirkland, Wash.
16. Mendonca, Kaysie. 12, Kaneohe, Hawaii.
17. Smith, Kim.* 13, Kirkland, Wash.
18. Soholt, Gillian.* 13, Kirkland, Wash.
19. Spahr, Alexis.* 14, Kirkland, Wash.
20. Powers, Jay.* 18, Kirkland, Wash.
21. Van Velzen, Eric.* 18, Bothell, Wash.

ADULTS

22. Baltuck, Naomi. Seattle, Wash. Teacher, storyteller.
23. Hill, Pat. Kirkland, Wash. Counselor, Seattle Girls' Choir Camp.
24. James, Billy Jo. Woodinville, Wash.
25. MacDonald, Margaret Read.* Kirkland, Wash. Counselor in Alaska, Puerto Rico, Washington.
26. Nehr, Julie.* Lynnwood, Wash. Grand Guardian, Job's Daughters.
27. Ribik, Kathleen.* Kirkland, Wash. Leader, Senior Troop, Girl Scouts.
28. Snyder, John. Snohomish, Wash. Teacher.

AMERICAN CAMPING ASSOCIATION MEMBERS

29. Hanson, Bob.* Fairfax, Calif. Mountain Camp II.
30. Herst, Bruce.* Bethesda, Md. Capital Camps.
31. Helm, Anne.* Louisville, Ky. YMCA Camp Piomongo.
32. Sindelar, Karen Antons.* McGregor, Minn. Camp New Hope.
33. Sindelar, Kevin A.* McGregor, Minn. Camp New Hope.
34. Trowbridge, Anne* and Kathy Steeber. Oregonia, Ohio. YMCA Camp Kern.
35. Updyke, Gloria.* York, Penn.

SCHOOLS, GROUPS

Some skits were collected in group interviews.

36. Cub Scout Troop, Edmonds, Wash.
37. The Community School,* Kirkland, Wash.
38. Quimper School, Olympic Peninsula, Wash.

Sources for Skits

The skit sources are arranged here just the way the skits are in this book. The contributors who shared the skits are represented by their numbers from the "Skit Contributor" list, and if they remembered where or when they saw a skit, I included that information too. For example. "YMCA Camp Orkila, 37, 1" means that contributors #37 (The Community School) and #1 (Susie Cameron) saw or heard a particular skit at Camp Orkila.

In some of these notes there is other information that helps us see where a skit idea may have come from, or how it could be used. For instance, contributors told me if they had heard of a skit idea used as a joke, or if they had seen it performed as an audience participation activity. This kind of information gives more insight about skits as folklore: how they travel, and the interesting ways people have changed them.

J.C. PENNEY'S CLOTHES: Burton Music Camp, 2; Boy Scouts, 17; YMCA, 18; American Legion (adults & children), 7; Seattle Girls' Choir, 13, 14; Camp Huston, Episcopal, 9; Outdoor Ed., 5th gr., 20; Job's Daughters, 26; 3; 19; Calif., 29; YMCA Camp Piomongo, Ky., YMCA Wis., 34.

THE REPORTER AT THE BRIDGE: Seattle Girls' Choir, 13, 14; Camp Seabeck, 18, 9, 7, 3; YMCA Day Camp, 19; Girl Scout Day Camp, 14 (also performed with cousins at grandparents' house); Northstar Jr. High School graduation, 14; Girl Scouts, 27; YMCA Camp Orkila, 37; Campfire, 22; Boy Scouts, 21; 20; 8; 1; Calif. (heard at least fifty times), 29; Camp Wyoming, Iowa, Camp Indian Sounds, Wis., 32; Scouts, Iowa, 33; YMCA Camp Piomongo, Ky., YMCA Wis. (favorite of

kids), 34; Pa., 35; Saint, *Campfire Stunts Two* p. 4 (collected in Surrey, Eng.).

THE POISON SPRING: YMCA Day Camp, 12; Eisenberg, *Fun With Skits*, p. 111; Harbin, *Skits, Plays, and Music*, p. 19; Harbin, *Fun Encyclopedia*, p. 239; Depew, *Cokesbury Party Book*, p. 192; Depew, *Cokesbury Stunt Book*, p. 104.

IS IT TIME YET?: YMCA Camp Orkila, 37, 1; Boy Scouts, 21; Community School, 5th gr., 19; Camp Moran, 17; Girl Scout Day Camp, 13, 14, 3; Outdoor Ed., 5th gr., 20; Calif., 29; Wis., 30; Iowa, Wis., 32; Iowa, 33; YMCA Ind., Wis., Ky., 34.

THE PICKPOCKET CONTEST: Seattle school, 22; Job's Daughters, 26.

THE KING'S ROYAL PAPERS: Girl Scout Day Camp, 3, 13, 14; YMCA Camp Orkila, 37; YMCA Day Camp, 19; Girl Scouts, 27; Campfire, Girl Scouts, 26; Calif., 29; Pa., 35; *Variant:* Set in office. Boss calls for important papers. Camp Wyoming, Iowa, 32; Camp Wyoming, Iowa, Boy Scouts, Iowa, 33; YMCA Ky., Wis., 34.

THE ELEVATOR: Community School, 5th gr., 19; Girl Scout Day Camp, 13, 14; Girl Scouts, 27; Campfire, Girl Scouts, 26; Outdoor Ed., 5th gr., 20; Iowa, 32, 33; YMCA Camp Piomongo, Ky., 34.

PRESENTS FOR THE TEACHER: Girl Scouts, 27; Job's Daughters, 26. My father, Murray Read, born 1902 in Southern Indiana, tells a similar joke, remembered from his youth, about a woman on a train with a basket of kittens.

SUBMARINE ATTACK: Camp Huston, Episcopal, 9, 14; YMCA Camp Orkila, 37; Girl Scouts, 27; Pa., 35; Saint, *Campfire Stunts Two,* p. 25 (collected in Surrey, Eng.).

THE AIRPLANE CRASH: Girl Scouts, 27.

THE SYMPATHETIC PATIENT: Girl Scouts, 27; Sunshine Girls Camp, Ind., (1956), 25; Boy Scouts, 21; 20; Calif., 29; Camp Wyoming, Iowa, 32; YMCA Ky., Wis., 34; Brings, *Master Stunt Book,* p. 57.

AT THE MOVIES: YMCA Day Camp, 19, 18; 37; Camp Moran, Boy Scouts, 17.

THE NAUGHTY STUDENT: Seattle Girls' Choir Camp, 13, 14, 16; YMCA Camp Orkila, 37.

THE FIRING SQUAD: YMCA Camp Orkila, 37; Boy Scouts, 21; Job's Daughters, 26; YMCA Wis., 34; Pa., 35.

THE MYSTERIOUS FLYING OBJECT: Girl Scouts, 27; Job's Daughters, 26; Outdoor Ed., 5th gr., 20; Wis., 30; YMCA Ky., Wis., 34; Eisenberg, *Omnibus,* p. 195.

THE CANDY CONTEST: Howard, *Complete Book,* p. 403.

BAILING OUT: Campfire, Girl Scouts, 26, 37; Iowa, 32, 33; *As joke only:* Mass., 30; Calif., 29.

THE ONE-ARMED BANDIT: YMCA Camp Orkila, 18; Boy Scouts, 21.

JOHNNY GOT RUN OVER BY A BUS: YMCA Camp Orkila, 37; Wis., 30; Camp Wyoming, Iowa, 32, 33 (chase cameraman off with pie). *Variant:* Cow is run over. YMCA Wis., 34.

THE EMPLOYMENT AGENCY: Girl Scout Day Camp, 14.

TREATING THE ACHE: Job's Daughters, 26; Brings, *Master Stunt Book,* p. 160.

THE BIGGEST LIARS IN TEXAS: Boy Scouts, 21; Job's Daughters, 26; Brings, *Master Stunt Book,* p. 158, p. 278.

GOODBYE IN ANY LANGUAGE: Central Washington University, 20; Outdoor Ed., 5th gr., 20; Depew, *Cokesbury Party Book,* p. 279.

IGOR KILL: Boy Scouts, 21; Campfire, Girl Scouts, 26; Calif., 29; Halter, "Skit Time," *Boy's Life,* June 1986, p. 42.

HOT NEWS: Outdoor Ed., 5th gr., 20; Job's Daughters, 26; Eisenberg, *Handbook of Skits,* p. 55.

THE VIPER IS COMING: Camp Huston, Episcopal, 9; Girl Scouts, 27; Job's Daughters, 26; 1; 9; 19; 5; Calif., 29; Wis., 30; Camp Holiday, N.H., Camp Wyoming, Iowa, 32; YMCA Camp Kern, Ohio, YMCA Wis., 34. *As a joke:* 9th gr. Camp, 20; Knapp, *One Potato,* p. 247.

AS CLEAN AS THREE RIVERS CAN GET IT: YMCA Camp Orkila, 37; Fort Flagler, 19; Girl Scouts, 27. *Variant:* As Clean As Ocean Can Get It, 18.

MINNIE MUSCLES: 20; Cub Scout "Skits and Puppets."

PICKING UP PEBBLES: Burton Music Camp, 2; Job's Daughters, 26; YMCA Indian Princesses, 13; Calif., 29; Loken, *Cheerleading*, p. 82. *Variant:* Girls return to camp after throwing "Pebbles" in the lake. YMCA Wis., 34.

THE FROGS GO WHEE!: Quimper School, 38; Camp Moran, Boy Scouts, 17; Campfire, Girl Scouts, 26; YMCA Day Camp, 18, Bob Herold, Northstar Jr. High teacher.

THE LITTLE ONE GOES WHEE!: YMCA Day Camp, 12; YMCA Camp Orkila, 37; Wis., 30; Camp Wyoming, Iowa, 32, 33; Camp Indian Sands, Wis., 32; YMCA Wis., YMCA Camp Kern, Ohio, 34.

"SHUT UP" AND HER DOG "TROUBLE": YMCA Day Camp, Hawaii, (1985), 16; Camp Moran, Boy Scouts, 17; Job's Daughters, 26; 13; 14; 18; 5; 1; Wis., Calif., 30.

THE FORTUNE TELLER: Camp Huston, Episcopal, 9, 14; Camp Silverton, Everett Schools, 36; YMCA Camp Orkila, 37; Job's Daughters, 26; Wis., 30.

THE CANDY STORE: Camp Moran, Boy Scouts, 17; Job's Daughters, 26; 20; Calif., 29; Ind., Wis., 34; Pa., 35; *Variant:* The cash register, counters, etc. are all played by dupes. Camp Wyoming, Iowa, 32, 33.

THE SQUIRREL'S HARVEST: Girl Scouts, 27; Job's Daughters, 26; Girl Scout Day Camp, 14; 20; Calif., 29 (very old); Camp Wyoming, Iowa, 32, 33; Harbin, *Fun Encyclopedia*, p. 234.

FISH MARKET CALLING: Girl Scouts, 27, 10; Job's Daughters, 26; 20; Calif., 29; Boy Scouts, Iowa, 33; Ind., Wis., 34; Pa., 35; Breen, *Party Book*, p. 114 (1939 version, holding up wire with magnetic properties which vibrates when people talk); Loken, *Cheerleading*, p. 81.

THE LIFE STORY OF TREES: Job's Daughters, 26; Girl Scouts, 27, 10; Seattle Girls' Choir Camp, 13, 14; Camp Riverdale, Ind., (1953) 25; Calif., 29; YMCA Ind., Ky., 34; Loken, *Cheerleading*, p. 82.

STARTING THE LAWN MOWER: YMCA Camp Orkila, 37; Boy Scouts, 21; Job's Daughters, 26; YMCA Wis., 34; Pa., 35.

THE ECHO: YMCA Day Camp, 12, 19, 18; Camp Moran, Boy Scouts, 17; Camp Seabeck, 7, 3; YMCA Camp Orkila, 37; Girl Scouts, 27; Boy Scouts, 21; Job's Daughters, 26; 20; Harbin, *New Fun Encyclopedia*, p. 27; Breen, *Party Book*, p. 334; MacFarlan, *Treasury*, p. 153.

THE HUMAN BONFIRE: Outdoor Ed., 5th gr., 13, 20. *Variant:* A house is built with human "logs" and catches fire. YMCA Ind., YMCA Wis., 34.

THE COFFEE SHOP TABLE: Camp Huston, Episcopal, 14, 9; YMCA Camp Orkila, 37; Quimper School, 38; Boy Scouts, 21; Job's Daughters, 26; Calif., 29, Wis., 30; Camp Wyoming, Iowa, 32, 33. *Variant:* Dupe is a lawnmower with a bowl of "gasoline" on back. Pa., 35.

THE UGLIEST MAN IN THE WORLD: Cub Scout Day Camp, 36; Girl Scouts, 27; YMCA Camp Orkila, 37, 8; Girl Scout Day Camp, 14; Boy Scouts, 21; Campfire, Girl Scouts, 26; Calif., 29 (very old); Camp Wyoming, Iowa, 32, 33; YMCA Camp Piomongo, Ky., Wis., 34; Pa., 35; Saint, *Campfire Stunts*, p. 22 (collected in Surrey, England).

OH-WA-TA-GOO-SIAM: Peter Kirk School, 6th gr., 13; Job's Daughters, 26; 1 (from her Uncle Henry); 20; 13; Calif., 29; 30 (from father who learned it at camp in Michigan in the 30s); YMCA Camp Piomongo, Ky., 34. *As initiation rite:* Camp Wyoming, 4H Camp, and Luther League, Iowa, 32; Boy Scouts, Iowa, 33.

THE TOOTHBRUSHERS: Camp Sambica, 4; YMCA Camp Orkila, 37.

THE EMPTY HEADS: Seattle Girls' Choir Camp, 23; Camp Huston, Episcopal, 9; Ky., 34.

GREEN HAIR: The Community School, 37; Pa., 34. As a joke: Mass., 29; Conn., 11. Variant: "How did you get such neat hair?" Iowa, 32, 33.

THE SUPER DUPER RAINBOW-FLAVORED BUBBLE GUM: Camp Huston, Episcopal, 9; Mountlake Terrace School, 2nd gr., 36; YMCA Camp Orkila, 37; Girl Scouts, 27, 10; Seattle Girls' Choir Camp, 6; YMCA Day Camp, 18; The Community School, 19; Girl Scout Camp, 7; 1; 14; 5; Calif., 29; Camp Wyoming, Iowa, 32, 33; YMCA Ky., Wis., 34; Pa., 35.

THE FLY: Camp Seabeck, 3; Woodside Elementary School, 2nd gr., 36; Girl Scouts, 27; Boy Scouts, 21; 18; 17; 14; Wis., 30.

GOT THE BEAT: 20; Iowa, 32, 33. As a joke: Conn., 11.

THE ZOOKEEPER AND HIS ANIMALS: Wis., 30 (Each cabin of campers represents one animal on stage; the narrator makes all perform); Howard, More Charades, p. 109.

THE SYMPATHETIC MOURNERS: Used as a skit, an audience participation activity, and a party game. Collected as a children's game in the American South. Harbin, Gay. p. 87 (old witch is dead); Breen, Party Book, p. 47 (Mrs. McGinty is dead); Mulac & Holmes, Party Game Book, p. 102 (Old Nick just went by); Harbin, Fun Encyclopedia, p. 212 (Aunt Dinah is dead, Tennessee children's game), p. 211 (Uncle Ned is dead); Knapp, One Potato, p. 147.

THE BUTTON FACTORY: Cub Scouts, 25; Hawaii, 16; Job's Daughters, 26; 1; YMCA Ky., Wis., 34 (chant "I am a factory worker"). Variant: Human machines, each camper adds an action. Md., 30.

THE VERY HUNGRY CATERPILLAR: Outdoor Ed., 5th gr., 3; YMCA Day Camp, 18; Boy Scouts, 21; Girl Scouts, 27; Campfire, Girl Scouts, 26; Girl Scout Day Camp, 13; Community School, 19; Camp Huston, Episcopal, 9; 1; Camp Wyoming and 4H Camp, Iowa, 32; N.H., 33; YMCA Ind., Minn., Ky., Wis., 34. Variant: Dragon. YMCA Camp Orkila, 37. Variant: Elephant made of two campers under blanket. Iowa, 32.

THE PET SLUG: Camp Huston, Episcopal, 9; Camp Seabeck, 3; YMCA Day Camp, 19; Boy Scouts, 21; 1.

THE ENLARGING WALL: Camp Huston, Episcopal, 9; Outdoor Ed., 5th gr., 7; YMCA Day Camp, 18; Boy Scouts, 21; Job's Daughters, 26; 3; Calif., 29; 25 (from Maryland friend, Marilyn Ribe). Variant: Enlarging machine. Iowa, 32, 33; YMCA Ky., Ohio, Wis., 34; Saint, Campfire Stunts Two, p. 15 (collected in Surrey, Eng.).

THE SPIT SKIT: Burton Music Camp, 2; Job's Daughters, 26; 1; Calif., 29; YMCA Camp Piomongo, Ky., 34.

THE FANCY PITCHERS: Heritage Christian School, 12; Job's Daughters, 26; Eisenberg, Fun with Skits, p. 81.

THE OPERATION: Job's Daughters, 26; Camp Riverdale, Methodist, Ind., (1956), Sunshine Girls Camp, Ind., (1958), Camp Rainbow Glacier, Alaska, (1960), 25; Harbin, Fun Encyclopedia, p. 212; Eisenberg, Handbook of Skits, p. 25; Thurston, Complete Book, p. 252; Feder, Clown Skits, pp. 143–147; Saint, Campfire Stunts, p. 29 (collected in Surrey, England).

HER SON'S OPERATION: Girl Scouts, 27; Job's Daughters, 26; Calif., 29 Harbin, New Fun Encyclopedia, p. 27; Carlson, Do It Yourself, p. 145.

FLORA THE DANCING FLEA: Job's Daughters, 26; Calif., 29; Camp Wyoming, Iowa (teacher claps and smashes flea), 32; Pa., 35; Eisenberg, Fun with Skits, p. 81.

THE SCRAMBLED MESSAGE: Outdoor Ed., 5th gr., 20; Campfire, Girl Scouts, 26; Clown Camp, Wis., 32; Iowa, 33; Eisenberg, *Omnibus*, p. 325.

THE EXERCISE KING: Camp Moran, Boy Scouts, 17; Outdoor Ed., 5th gr., 20; Campfire, Girl Scouts, 26; Iowa, 32; 33; YMCA Camp, Pa., 35.

THE EXERCISE LESSON: Burton Music Camp, 2; Outdoor Ed., 5th gr., 21; Job's Daughters, 26; 1; 8; 14.

THE BEAUTY LESSON: Seattle Girls' Choir Camp, 13, 14; Outdoor Ed., 5th gr., 21, 20; Job's Daughters, 26; 1; 8; Wis., 34; Iowa, 32, 33.

THE COOKING LESSON: Job's Daughters, 26; 20; 1; 8; Wis., 34.

THE BIG DATE: Burton Music Camp, 2; Outdoor Ed., 5th gr., 21; Job's Daughters, 26; 20; 8; 5; Pa., 30; Iowa, Wis., 32; Iowa, 33.

THE DINNER DATE: Job's Daughters, 26; Boy Scouts, 21. *Mixed-up Bodies Variants:* Getting dressed and eating breakfast. YMCA Ky., Wis., 34; Pa., 35; Iowa, 32, 33; Saiht, *Campfire Stunts*, p. 31 (collected in Surrey, Eng.).

DANCING KNEE DOLLS: Job's Daughters, 26; Eisenberg, *Omnibus*, p. 327.

CHIN FACES: Boy Scouts, 21; 8; Iowa, 32; Ky. (from Oregon counselor), 34.

STOMACH FACES: Cruise ship, 36; 8.

THE LIGHTHOUSE KEEPER'S DAUGHTER: Church social, 24; Seattle Girls' Choir Camp, 14; Calif., 29; Thurston, *Complete Book*, p. 253; Eisenberg, *Handbook of Skits*, p. 116; Carlson, *Act It Out*, p. 44 (princess in castle, witch); Preston, *Modern Stunt Book*, p. 42 (includes gestures for audience).

WHO'LL PAY THE RENT?: Girl Scouts, 27; Camp Moran, Boy Scouts, 17; Boy Scouts, 21; 13; 20; 5; 19 (dialogue popular in junior high school: "You must pay the rent!" etc.); Calif., 29; Wis., 30; YMCA Wis. 32; Breen, *Party Book*, p. 335; Thurston, *Complete Book*, p. 246; Mulac, *Party Game Book*, p. 108; Yates, *Western Folklore*, Jan. 1951, p. 59 ("Most people have heard this chant"). *As audience participation activity led by one person:* Boy Scouts, 21; Calif., 19; Wis., 32; Camp Wyoming, Iowa, Vt., and N.J. 32, 33; Wis., 34; Pa., 35.

"AH": Harbin, *New Fun Encyclopedia*, p. 45; Eisenberg, *Handbook of Skits*, p. 116.

THE SESAME STREET BUS: Seattle Girls' Choir Camp, 13, 14; Job's Daughters, 26; Boy Scouts, 21; 5; Wis., 34.

DR. BLUEBONNET: Job's Daughters, 26; 4.

TAKES A LICKIN' AND KEEPS ON TICKIN': 25.

YELLOW FINGERS: 34, Ohio.

ABEL'S FABLE: Girl Scouts, 27; Campfire, Girl Scouts, 26; 30, Md. *As a joke:* Cub Scouts, 25.

TAKING THE PENGUINS FOR A RIDE: Campfire, Girl Scouts, 26; The Community School, 37; Boy Scouts, 21. *As a joke:* Jones, *Laughter in Appalachia*, p. 107.

THE GHOST OF THE TWO WHITE EYES: Girl Scouts, 27. *As a joke:* Cub Scouts, 25; Knapp, *One Potato*, p. 246.

STRANDED IN THE DESERT: YMCA Camp Orkila, 37; Boy Scouts, 21; YMCA Wis., 34; YMCA Camp, Pa., 35.

STONE SOUP: Boy Scouts, 21; 2nd gr., 1; N.H., 32; Pa., 35; *As a popular children's folktale.* MacDonald, *Storyteller's Sourcebook*, motif K112.2.

THE WIDE-MOUTHED FROG: Boy Scouts, 21; Calif., 29; Iowa, 32, 33; YMCA Camp, Wis., 34. *As a humorous anecdote,* 25; Schneider, *The Wide-Mouthed Frog.*

THE TWIST-MOUTH FAMILY: Seattle Girls' Choir Camp, 14; Girl Scouts, Ind. (1950s), 25; Calif., 29 (old, college-educated son snuffs out candle with fingers); Carlson, *Do It*, p. 47. As a folktale, "The Snooks Family". MacDonald, *Storyteller's Sourcebook*, motif X131.

THE BAD EXCHANGE: Seattle Girls' Choir Camp, 25; Korty, *Silly Soup*, p. 40; As a folktale: MacDonald, *Storyteller's Sourcebook*, motif N255.8.

THE WISE MAN: 30 (a Hasidic story). As a folktale: MacDonald, *Storyteller's Sourcebook*, motif Z49.16.

THE MOTHER GOOSE SINGERS: Outdoor Ed., 5th gr., 20; Breen, *Party Book*, p. 343. *Variants:* Chorus, "The window, the window, the second-story window. If you can't sing a rhyme and tell it on time, we'll throw it out the window." YMCA Camp, Minn., 34;. As *song only:* Chorus, "The window, the window, the second story window. High low, low high, she threw it out the window", Md., 30.

HUMP-TE-DUMP RAP: The Community School, 37.

PRESENTS FOR YOU!: Howard, *Complete Book*, p. 533.

THE PET ROCKS PERFORM: Camp Moran, Boy Scouts, 17; Camp Huston, Episcopal, 9, 14.

A-BOOM-CHIC-A-BOOM!: YMCA Camp Orkila, 37; Girl Scouts, 27; Girl Scout Day Camp, 13, 14; Boy Scouts, 21; 20; 1; YMCA Camp Piomongo, Ky., YMCA Camp Kern, Ohio, YMCA Camp, Wis., 34. *Audience participation only:* Wis., 30; Calif., 29; Iowa, 32, 33; YMCA Camp, Pa., 35.

I'M A LITTLE TEAPOT: Washington State University, 15; Boy Scouts, 21; 14; 1; 5. As a song only: Wis., 30; YMCA, Ind., 34.

MIXED SINGING: 25.

THE UPSIDE DOWN SINGERS: Depew, *Cokesbury Party Book*, p. 333.

MIXED BODY SINGING: YMCA Camp Piomongo, Ky., 34.

THE LIVING XYLOPHONE: 8; Iowa, 32; Eisenberg, *Omnibus*, p. 297.

BALLOON ORCHESTRA: Harbin, *Fun Encyclopedia*, p. 47.

THE ONE MAN BAND: 20; 10; Eisenberg, *Omnibus*, p. 298.

SOUR NOTES: Burton Music Camp, 2; Howard, *Complete Book*, p. 117–118; Thurston, *Complete Book*, p. 237.

THE KITCHEN BAND: Senior Center, Bothell, Wash. 25; Wis., Pa., 30; Iowa, 32, 33; YMCA Camp Piomongo, Ky., 34.

HEART AND SOUL: Olympic Music Camp, 10.

THE PAPER BAG BAND: Olympic Music Camp, 10.

Acknowledgments

Thanks to all who contributed skits to this project. I am especially grateful to the following individuals, who read through my entire skit list, checking those skits they had seen in performance. Most of the skits in this book were contributed from the repertoire of these campers and counselors:

Head teacher Lynn Black, and the fifth and sixth graders at The Community School in Kirkland, Washington; Kathleen Ribik, leader, and Girl Scout Troop #1401, Kirkland, Washington; Eric Van Velzen, Eagle Scout, Bothell, Washington; Julie Nehr, Job's Daughters, Mountlake Terrace, Washington; Northstar Junior High School students Dominique Jordan, Lisa Kester, Emily Drew, Kim Smith, Gillian Soholt, and Julie MacDonald of Kirkland, Washington; Youth Theatre Northwest students Susie Cameron, Wendy Herlich, Tova Dodge, Heather Karnes, Jennifer MacDonald, and Nathan Dodge; Bothell Library patrons Tanya Lee, Kerry Downey, and Anthony Long; and Jay Powers of Central Washington University.

I was impressed by the great help offered by members of the American Camping Association, who took time to read my long list of skits and send notes on the favorites in their own camps. Thanks to Bob Hanson, Bruce Herst, Anne Helm, Karen and Kevin Sindelar, Kathy Steeber, Anne Trowbridge, and Gloria Updyke.

Special thanks to my editor, Diantha Thorpe, to her daughter, Elizabeth Thorpe and to Nancy Boyles and her students in the Creative Learning Program, North Haven Public Schools, Connecticut, for field testing some of these skits.

Bibliography

Boy Scouts of America. *Skits and Puppets*. New Brunswick, N.J.: Boy Scouts of America, 1963.

Breen, Mary J. *The Party Book*. Prepared for the National Recreation Association. New York: A.S. Barnes, 1939.

Brings, Lawrence. *Master Stunt Book*. Minneapolis, Minn. : T.S. Dennison, 1956.

Carlson, Bernice Wells. *Do It Yourself: Tricks, Stunts, and Skits*. Nashville, Tenn.: Abingdon, 1952.

———. *Act It Out*. Nashville, Tenn.: Abingdon, 1956.

Cub Scout "Skits and Puppets." Pow Wow, North Lakes District Roundtable, 1977.

Depew, Arthur M. *The Cokesbury Stunt Book*. New York: Abingdon-Cokesbury, 1934.

———. *The Cokesbury Party Book*. Nashville, Tenn.: Abingdon, 1959.

Eisenberg, Helen and Larry Eisenberg. *Fun with Skits, Stunts, and Stories*. New York: Association Press, 1955.

———. *The Handbook of Skits and Stunts*. Martinsville, Ind.: American Camping Association, 1984.

———. *The Omnibus of Fun*. New York: Association Press, 1956.

Feder, Happy Jack. *Clown Skits for Everyone*. New York: Arco, 1984.

Halligan, Terry. *Funny Skits and Sketches*. New York: Sterling, 1987.

Halter, Jon C. "Skit Time." *Boy's Life*, 42–43, June 1986.

Harbin, E.O. *Fun Encyclopedia*. Nashville, Tenn.: Abingdon, 1940.

———. *Gay Parties for All Occasions*. Nashville, Tenn.: Abingdon, 1950.

———. *The NEW Fun Encyclopedia*. v. 4. Revised by Bob Sessions. Nashville, Tenn.: Abingdon, 1984.

Howard, Vernon. *The Complete Book of Children's Theater*. Garden City, N.Y.: Doubleday, 1969.

———. *More Charades and Pantomimes*. New York: Sterling, 1961.

Ireland, Norma Olin. *An Index to Skits and Stunts*. Boston: F.W. Faxon, 1958.

Jones, Loyal and Billy Edd Wheeler. *Laughter in Appalachia: A Festival of Southern Mountain Humor*. Little Rock, Ark.: August House, 1987.

Knapp, Mary and Herbert Knapp. *One Potato, Two Potato . . . : The Secret Education of American Children.* New York: Norton, 1976.

Korty, Carol. *Silly Soup: Ten Zany Plays with Songs and Ideas for Making Them Your Own.* New York: Scribner's, 1977.

Loken, Newt. *Cheerleading.* New York: Ronald, 1945.

MacDonald, Margaret Read. *The Storyteller's Sourcebook: A Subject, Title, and Motif Index to Folklore Collections for Children.* Detroit, Mich: Neal-Schuman/Gale Research, 1982.

MacFarlan, Allan C. *Treasury of Memory-Making Campfires.* New York: Association Press, 1963.

Mason, Bernard S. and Elmer D. Mitchell. *Party Games for All.* New York: Barnes & Noble, 1946.

Mechling, Jay. "The Magic of the Boy Scout Campfire," *Journal of American Folklore.* 93 (367); 35–56, Jan.-March 1980.

Mulac, Margaret E. and Marian S. Holmes. *The Party Game Book.* New York: Harper, 1951.

Preston, Effa E. *Fun With Skits.* Minneapolis, Minn.: T.S. Dennison, 1956.

Preston, Effa E., Beatrice Plumb, and Harry W. Githens. *The Modern Stunt Book: A Collection of Stunts and Skits for Teen Ages, Adults, and Grammar Grades.* Minneapolis, Minn.: T.S. Dennison, 1945.

Saint, David. *Campfire Stunts.* Surrey, England: Printforce, n.d.

———. *Campfire Stunts Two.* Surrey, England: Printforce, n.d.

Schneider, Rex. *The Wide-Mouthed Frog.* Owings Mills, Md.: Stemmer House, 1980.

Schwartz, Alvin. *Scary Stories to Tell in the Dark.* New York: Lippincott, 1981.

Thurston, LaRue A. *The Complete Book of Campfire Programs.* New York: Association Press, 1958.

Yates, Norris. " Children's Folk Plays in Western Oregon." *Western Folklore,* 10 (1): 55–59, January 1951.

Subject Index

Add a Skit

Do you know a great skit that didn't get into this book? If you have seen a skit which we missed please write and tell us about it. Include your name, age, hometown, and the place and year you saw the skit (if you remember that). If we hear about a lot of fun skits that didn't get into this book, we just might make another skit book, one with skits from kids all over. And, if we use your skit, we will list you as a contributor.

Send skit ideas to: THE SKIT BOOK
                        c/o Linnet Books
                        PO Box 4327
                        Hamden, Connecticut 06514

Performance Notes